CALL ME ELLA

A Memoir

JOAN E. KAUFMAN

Copyright © 2013 by Joan E. Kaufman. ALL RIGHTS RESERVED. No part of this book may be reproduced or transmitted in any form by any means, electronic or mechanical, including photocopying and recording, or by any information storage and retrieval systems, except as may be expressly permitted in writing from the author. Requests for permission should be addressed to joanekaufman@aol.com.

ISBN-13: 978-1494713997
ISBN-10: 1494713993

Some names and identifying details have been changed to protect the privacy of individuals.

DEDICATION

This book is dedicated to my family — by birth, adoption and marriage. I would like to give a special thank you to my dear friend and new "cuz" Elaine, the woman who believed in me and helped me learn who I am and where I came from.

JOAN E. KAUFMAN

PROLOGUE

"It's all starting to make sense now."

"What's making sense now?" Brad asks.

"How long have you been standing there?" I carefully shift some papers out of the way to make room for my husband to sit down and join me. Patting my newspaper-cluttered bed I smile and add, "I hadn't realized I said that out loud."

"So, you make a habit of sitting alone talking to yourself?"

"I just can't get over the secrets. And all those lies they told me, and everyone else, to hide the story of my birth. It's hard to believe Mom and Dad never talked about … That they actually went to their graves without …"

"We really don't know what your parents told their friends and relatives. They've all passed away. We just know they kept you in the dark."

"They did a really good job, that's for sure. Although, looking back, there were clues."

"Like the time your mom shot her foot through the kitchen wall?" I'm impressed Brad remembered that.

"I did think she was over-reacting to my simple question, 'Do you know anything about my birth mother?'"

"I guess now we know why she reacted so violently."

"Mom always used to tell me I was too sensitive. Maybe she was sensitive as well." I take a deep breath as my husband wraps me tightly in his arms. "I know you're right. At some point I need to let go. I need to forgive my mom for lying about my adoption. I'm just not ready yet. Can you understand my feeling that way?"

Brad nods and gazes at the mess on the bed. "OK, I give. What's all this?"

"Look! This is the scrapbook I was telling you about." As carefully as if I was examining the original Bill of Rights at the National Archives, I open the collection of dog-eared newspaper clippings my brother, my brother, gave me, and point to, without touching, one of the yellowed pages.

"Wow! Look at these scores!" Brad begins shaking his head as he reads aloud scorecards hand-tallied in the days before automation. "Unbelievable: 260, 279, 300! I can't even imagine a perfect game!"

"I know. These would be series scores for us."

"If we were lucky."

"My brother. A professional bowler. I wonder if I ever saw him on TV." I sigh.

"What's the matter?"

"I have a brother." I wipe a tear from my eye. "I have a brother."

"And I now have a brother-in-law! Cool."

I start gathering the pages of the scrapbook, preparing to find a safe place to store them.

"Your mind should be at ease now that you have the answers you've been looking for. Maybe now you can relax a little?" Brad asks.

"I have most of the answers. Not all. Those were some secrets we uncovered. Weren't they? Who would have guessed my birth involved illegal gambling? Or cheating spouses?"

Brad gets up from the bed and walks to the door. Turning toward me he adds,

"Like the word "cancer" was never uttered back "in the day", infidelity was swept under the bed as well, everyone pretending it never happened. My wife's story, The Godfather meets Goodfellas. Brandon would love how The Mob played a role in your birth." He laughs at his own joke. "Let it go for a while. I'm starved. Want to go out for dinner?"

"I'm sorry. I still keep thinking about how my life would have been different if my parents had told me the truth. I would have understood."

"I know. However, at some point you really need to put your adoption behind you and move on."

"I will. Just not yet. I've got to do one more thing."

"What's that?"

"I need to tell my brother how I found him."

CHAPTER ONE

I killed her!

What else was I to think when Mom told me my birth mother died during childbirth? Without knowing any details, I spent countless hours imagining what happened the night I was born. The night I was given up for adoption. I couldn't help wondering what my birth mother's last moments were like before she died.

By the time I was ten, I started writing my story. I never got very far, tearing up page after page, changing the scenarios. Propped up on my elbows on my bed, pen in hand, I'd stare at my floral wallpaper, concentrating, waiting for the words to magically appear on the page, establishing a beginning for my life. I'd write a few lines then rip the sheet from my loose leaf notebook, crumple it up, toss it in the general direction of my wastebasket, and start again. To this day, I'm still making up stories, trying to understand my birth. Only now, I make the changes on my laptop. That's much easier.

This is the version I'm working on...

Lightning struck outside her hospital window, momentarily highlighting the woman's pained face. Relieved she was no longer lying in a pool of blood, the new mother struggled to lift her head off the pillow, hoping to gain the nurse's sympathy.

"This is against hospital rules," the nurse whispered from the doorway, her eyes scanning the laundry bins and empty gurneys lining the dimly lit hallway as if she were a secret agent on the lookout for spies. Clutching the tiny bundle to the bib of her starched white uniform, the nurse approached the bed guardedly. "I could lose my job if someone catches you with the baby you are putting up for adoption."

This account has possibilities, but it needs work. I need to explain why a nurse would risk losing her job for a patient. Maybe she knew the woman didn't have long to live and she wanted to grant a dying woman her last wish.

There must be some exception for a new mother who wants to see her child, the nurse thought. *To say goodbye to her baby, her flesh and blood, her daughter. Rules are made for a reason*, the nurse reminded herself. *Why should I risk my job for a woman I never met before? A woman I will never see again. What if she is going to die? She's lost so much blood. I can't turn my back on a dying woman, can I?*

That's better. I reach for my mug of cold, stale coffee. Ignoring the dregs floating to the top, I take another sip. It's getting late but I want to finish this part at least. Now, let's see if the story makes sense.

After blotting her tear soaked face with the bed sheet, the mother extended her arms, begging, "Just for a moment. I promise I'll give her right back."

Still torn between following hospital policy and doing what she felt was right, the nurse hesitated, clutching the tightly wrapped infant to her breast.

"Please let me hold her for just a moment..."

Before they take her away forever.

The nurse finally gave in.

Cradling the infant against her swollen breast, synching her breathing with the steady rhythm of the newborn's heartbeat, there was a moment, a fleeting second, when the woman considered changing her mind. Noticing the baby's eyelids flutter, she questioned how she could have ever agreed to give up this precious gift. As the woman brushed her lips against the child's forehead, she felt a gentle tug. Glancing down at the perfectly formed hand, a miniature version of her own, gripping her pinky, she was torn, not wanting to let go.

As hot tears continued streaming from the new mother's eyes, she sensed the nurse hovering impatiently, waiting to rip her flesh and blood from her arms. For the second time in one evening, the mother knew loss as her childless limbs, now weightless, rose on their own. Although her heart was broken, she knew there was no turning back. It was the right thing to do.

Why do I always picture my birth taking place on a stormy night? For all I know I could have been born on a beautiful, sunny day. I'm being overly melodramatic. A real Sara Bernhard, like my adoptive parents used to call me. Nevertheless, something doesn't feel right. This version assumes my birth mother planned to give me up for adoption. Mom told me I was adopted because she died.

Maybe the story should begin: *No longer lying in a pool of blood, the young mother begged to hold her baby, just once, knowing she didn't have long to live.*

Yes. That's better. It assumes my birth mother wanted to keep me, but had to give me up for adoption because she knew she was going to die, not because she didn't want me. Not because she didn't love me.

I don't remember being told I was adopted. As other children know they came from their mommy's "tummy", I always understood I came from another woman's tummy. My birth story didn't involve a run to a hospital. When Mom told me, "We picked you," it sounded to me as if I were an item on her shopping list. I pictured baby me, lying quietly in a pink bassinet at the A&P, perhaps next to a stack of starched white cotton diapers and jars of Gerber baby food. I imagined my tiny hands grasping an old worn out rattle from the orphanage. I saw myself laying quietly, hoping, praying that one of the nice couples would pick me up and place me in their cart.

In reality, I always knew some stranger, someone I had never met, gave me life, and then died. I wanted to know more. Therefore, every once in a while I'd ask Mom the same question, "Do you know anything about my birth?"

Her answer, "All I know is, she died", never satisfied me. Eventually, I started wondering if Mom was deliberately keeping something from me. Maybe she was protecting me, for my own good. What if I was the product of rape? Or what if she knew my birth mother just wanted to get rid of me. Or worse, what if Dad found me in the dumpster behind his butcher shop?

I guess I just wanted to be reassured I wasn't a mistake. Mom could have simply said, "It doesn't matter how you came to be. The important thing is that we are so lucky to have you." Yes, that would have been a better answer. However, I would still have had many unanswered questions.

I never asked my dad.

CHAPTER TWO

Nineteen fifty-four was a year of change. The Supreme Court's ruling in Brown v. Board of Education determined that segregation in US Public Schools was unconstitutional. Rosa Parks' arrest in Montgomery, Alabama, set the American Civil Rights Movement in motion. Senator Joseph R. McCarthy continued his witch hunt for communist sympathizers. Elvis Presley began his music career. *Lord of the Flies* and *The Lord of the Rings* were topping the charts. Swanson introduced TV Dinners. And *I Love Lucy* was the #1 rated show on TV.

I didn't know how the *I Love Lucy* show would affect my life.

When Mom said, "Daddy's tired, don't bother him," I didn't ask questions.

I finished setting the kitchen table with the brown floral everyday dishes Mom bought at the A&P. Our good china was only used on holidays, when we ate in the dining room. I set one large dinner plate on each of the three orange plastic placemats on the round wood-grained Formica table. To the left of each plate, I centered a fork on the paper napkin I folded in a triangular shape. To the right of the plate I laid a knife, the blade side facing the plate, and a teaspoon to the right of the knife. I always made sure to get this arrangement correct so Mom wouldn't get upset. Or, maybe I should say, so she wouldn't get any more upset than she already was. She'd been stirring her soup for quite a while now, pretending to keep busy. I know she's staring out the window, wondering where Dad is. Why he's so late. I sit cross-legged on my swivel chair at the table, trying to look busy, as I watch Mom's routine, the same one I see every night. Stirring the soup, pretending nothing is wrong. Checking the breaded veal cutlet, or the pot roast, in the covered pan on the stove, hoping it hasn't dried out.

"Where is Daddy?" Mom asks, glancing over at me for a second before she looks back out the window. I know she's not expecting an answer. I don't dare ask to start dinner or take a bite of the rye bread before Dad gets home. She'd tell me that would spoil my dinner.

As the sun sets and the sky darkens, Mom rests the soup ladle on a bowl and comes over to join me at the table. We both wait to hear "The Beast", which is much noisier than Mom's car "The Beauty", pull into the driveway. Watching Mom worry makes me start to worry. *Is he all right? What if he was in an accident?*

At last, Koko, my brown standard French poodle, barks and runs to the front door signally a car is pulling up in the driveway. All is well. Mom and I get back into action and start to bring the food to the table. When Dad's late like this, there's no time to waste. I know Mom wants to serve right away so we can get this meal over with and she can clean the kitchen. In minutes, the three of us are seated at the table with Mom complaining, "I don't want to hear a word about dinner being dry. It was perfect an hour ago."

I don't know why Mom never asks Dad why he is late getting home. She just takes her seat, dishes out the chicken, potatoes and peas, placing only one small piece of chicken on her plate. "Go ahead, start eating," Mom insists, not taking a bite of her own meal. Instead, she stares at me. I know she's watching how I'm going to handle the food on my plate. I'm sure I'll do something wrong. I always do.

I glance sideways, noticing Mom's frosted hair. Perfectly coiffed at the beauty parlor every Saturday, her "do" stays in place all week, like a stiff helmet, until she gets it redone. She asks me to go with her on Saturday to get my hair frosted like hers. None of the kids in school have frosted hair. That's for older women. I say "no."

I start breathing harder but I don't want her to notice that she's getting to me. I won't let myself cry. That's really stupid to do when I'm not in pain. But sometimes I can't help it. Sometimes she just starts yelling at me for nothing, right in front of him. When I can't hold back my tears, even though I squeeze my eyes really hard trying to keep them inside, that's the time my dad speaks up. "Better stop right now or I'll give you something to cry about," he always says. That makes me mad at him. Doesn't he hear her yelling at me? Criticizing me? Why doesn't he understand I already have something to cry about? I know he means business since a big part of his job at home is teaching me a lesson. Not tonight though. I keep quiet. I don't let him see me cry.

I never really see Mom eat. She mostly picks at her food, or takes nothing at all. She has coffee and a cigarette for breakfast while I have my Cream of Wheat. Sometimes, for lunch, she spoons a little bit of cottage cheese on dry toast and nibbles on that while I eat the salami on rye, or the peanut butter and jelly on Pepperidge Farm bread that she made for me. She must eat more when I'm not around, because she's not thin. I mentioned that once, when she was telling me how fat I was, but she said she was thin when she was my age. That's what counts. I never mentioned her weight again. She brings up mine all the time.

I'm supposed to sit quietly at the table until Mom pours her coffee and lights her cigarette. After she inhales deeply, I wait for the signal, a wave of her manicured hand in the air, like a movie star dismissing her servants, which tells me it's time to get up and start clearing the dishes. Until that time, I wait. I try to follow her rules. I really do.

Mom sits straight up in her seat, no elbows on the table, carefully lifting her coffee cup from its saucer with her pinky finger extended, pointing high up in the air. I try not to roll my eyes as I picture her thinking she's dining with the Queen. Or, maybe she thinks she is the Queen.

"Why are you eating all your peas at once?" Mom says. I know it's a statement, not a question. Without waiting for a response, she tells me for the zillionth time, "Take a forkful of peas, then go on to your potatoes and then your meat." Big sigh.

I try not to make eye contact with her. Like they tell us not to look directly at a stray dog, I know looking at her could make her angrier. Although not looking at her might seem rude. And I know she's already upset that Dad was late. I'm not really sure what to do. Why can't she just let me eat my food the way I want? Peas are my favorite. Sometimes I mash them in my baked potato hoping to hear the popping sound it makes. Then Mom says I shouldn't play with my food. I don't say anything about the way she eats.

I glance over at Dad, wondering why he doesn't stick up for me. Is he staying out of this because he's tired, or is he afraid of her, just like I am? I know I shouldn't say anything, but as usual, I have trouble keeping my opinions to myself. "I like to finish all my peas first. This is the way I eat." I whisper. It doesn't matter if I speak softly or yell. To Mom, I'm talking back. If it wasn't the peas, she would be criticizing how I eat my potatoes, or part my hair or tie my shoes. No matter what I do, she would do it differently, and she lets me know it. What sets Mom off the most at dinner, however, is how I always put ketchup on my chicken. And this meal is no different.

"Andre, do you see what your daughter is doing?" Mom says to deaf ears. Dad is just happy to have a chance to sit down. I know he's had a long day. I'm not supposed to bother him with anything that's on my mind.

Mom hasn't put a bite of food in her mouth yet as she carefully monitors my intake. After Dad finishes buttering his rye bread, he looks up to respond, "No honey child," what is Joanie doing?"

"She's ruining my chicken."

He knows better than to argue with her. "Don't upset your mother," Dad tells me, obviously trying to avoid a fight.

"I get no respect." Mom returns her fork to her plate, not wanting to end this conversation. She sounds just like Rodney Dangerfield, the comedian on the Ed Sullivan show Sunday night. When he said "I get no respect" everyone laughed. I know I shouldn't laugh.

I want to throw my plate on the floor screaming, "Don't tell me how to eat! If I didn't eat it with ketchup, I wouldn't eat it at all," and then stomp out of the room showing Mom she can't bully me all the time, but I'd probably get killed for that. Besides, I'd be hungry later and I wouldn't be able to sneak back into the kitchen for hours, not until after *The Johnny Carson Show*, when they are both watching TV.

By ten years old, I'm getting smarter. Trying hard to avoid another fight, I quietly pick up my plate, fork and napkin, and move to the TV room. Resting the remains of my dinner on a metal TV tray, I tune in our black and white Zenith to *I Love Lucy*. I can't take Mom's criticizing anymore. As I do most nights of the week now, I pretend Lucy is my real mom and I'm living in a world in which I can do no wrong.

Curled up on the cozy, well-worn leather club chair, I try to tune out Mom's ranting, although I can't stop thinking about what just happened. What always happens. If it wasn't the ketchup, she'd be pointing out something else I was doing wrong. "Sit up straight", she'd say. Or, "elbows off the table"; or her ever popular, "I told you it's not liver, eat it." Mostly it's the ketchup that pisses her off. I don't really care if she thinks I'm ruining her stupid chicken anyway. When I grow up I'm going to eat all the ketchup I want.

Why can't Mom just let me eat my dinner in peace? I wonder, noticing how Lucy never criticizes Little Ricky. I can still hear Mom ranting and raving in the kitchen. I give her a few minutes to stop before I get up to shut the door and relax, escaping reality in the welcoming electronic bosom of my "other mother". My 19 inch, black and white, perfect mother. Lucille Ball, my red-headed fantasy mom, is always there for me, calming me down. Sometimes I wish she was my real mom. Or June Cleaver or Donna Reed. I bet they let their children eat ketchup. Why does she even buy the ketchup if I'm not allowed to eat it?

I love my TV shows. Especially my favorite, *I Love Lucy*. For one-half hour each day I pretend I'm no longer the butcher's adopted child. I am the daughter of a famous night club entertainer living in the lap of luxury in a chic New York apartment. I'm no longer an ungrateful, milk spilling, klutz; I am Lucy's miracle daughter, the child who could do no wrong. Crying each time I watch the episode in which Lucy tells Ricky she is pregnant, I pretend this is my history. My birth story. I believe Ricky's tears of joy are for me as he wraps his arms around his wife singing, *"We're Having a Baby"*.

I notice the kitchen quieting down as I push my empty plate to the side and continue staring at the screen. After Dad finishes dinner he comes in and joins me, lying on the couch. We sit in silence, watching Walter Cronkite reporting the nightly body counts from Vietnam, until he falls asleep. Then I change the channel.

***

Mom never understood why I asked about my birth. Why should she? Most people spend little time thinking about the circumstances of their birth. They take it for granted. But when you're adopted, you're constantly reminded. From the first time I was asked, "What was life like in the orphanage?" to my third grade teacher introducing us to the idea of genetics, I thought about how I came to be. Our assignment, to make a family tree and put a star by everyone on the tree who had our eye color, seemed like a waste of time for me. *My parents just picked me up at the hospital,* I thought. *I don't have anyone's eyes.*

As I grew older, each time I went to a new doctor, they'd

ask for my medical history. My answer, "I don't have one, I'm adopted," ended that line of questioning. For me, it didn't matter that my father died of heart failure. That my mother succumbed to cancer. They don't care if anyone in my family has had diabetes or inflammatory bowel disease. I have no medical history. I'm always starting with a fresh slate.

As a child I couldn't put into words why I was curious about the events that occurred on those days, months, before Mom and Dad mailed out the engraved birth announcements proclaiming: baby girl, 6 pounds.

All I knew about being adopted was my parents weren't involved in my actual conception and birth. But what about the rest of the story? Where were they when they got the call? Did they pick me up from the hospital? What hospital? Did they want a girl? Were they disappointed I wasn't a boy? Did they meet my birth mother before she died? Was she pretty? Did a social worker hand me to them? Were they excited? Everyone has a story, don't they? There's nothing wrong with wanting my own story. "You were adopted. We picked you." That's not enough information.

Looking back now, I can see where I went wrong. I wasn't specific enough in my questioning. Instead of asking Mom the general, open ended, question, "Do you know anything about my birth?" I should have sat both my parents down, shone a light in their eyes and said, "What happened on the night of August 30? And please, do not leave out any of the details."

In the beginning, I guess I just wanted to know if I had actually spent time at an orphanage. So the answer, "We brought you home from the hospital", was enough. As I got older, I wondered if Andre and Sylvia had tried to start a family for years, planning and praying for a child, saddened to learn they were infertile. It upset me how whenever I'd ask Mom about my birth, she never used the words "love" or "longing" in her: "You were adopted. We picked you," answer. I wanted to find out if my dad would have had better answers for me but I knew not to bother him. Mom was the one who made decisions, answered questions. Dad, always tired, or busy, was to be left alone. I understood that.

I'm sure my questions must have seemed insensitive to Mom's feelings. How could I have been so ungrateful for everything she'd done for me? I should have said, "I love you and I'm so glad you are my mother," before adding, "but I just want to know a little more about the woman who gave me up and why you adopted me. Please help me fill in the blanks." How should I, as a ten year old, have explained to the woman who cooked my dinner, washed my clothes and schlepped me to piano lessons, why I wanted to know something about another woman who was able to get pregnant when she was not? Having unanswered questions didn't get easier as I got older. Why couldn't I have just let it alone?

No, I had the right to ask. All children ask, Why is the sky is blue? Why shouldn't I touch a hot stove? And definitely, *Where did I come from?* Always feeling I was missing some important information, I wouldn't let go.

CHAPTER THREE

The kitchen phone rang in the middle of the day. Andre, finishing his bagel sandwich, answered it within seconds. So excited by the news he cried out to Sylvia, "It's time," leaving the handset dangling from its cord as he ran to the front hall closet to grab their coats.

"Where's the fire?" I imagined Sylvia saying, knowing full well the baby wasn't going anywhere. "They'll wait."

Mom always made Dad wait as she applied a final coat of lipstick and hairspray. In their late model Buick, Andre and Sylvia would undoubtedly argue over directions, each insisting his or her shortcut is better than the other's, as usual. Finally, with no immediate urgency, they would make their grand entrance into the hospital's marble-tiled lobby. Mom, wearing her "summer weight" mink coat, and Dad, undoubtedly sporting his signature suit and bowtie. Having furnished the nursery with the finest crib and most luxurious satin bedding, they were ready to start their new life.

Yes, the day they brought their baby girl home from the hospital must have been memorable. Even exciting. Why couldn't Mom share this with me? Instead of repeating, "That's all I know.

Don't ask me any more questions!" until I finally got the hint.

I let my adoption define me. Always stewing somewhere in the back of my mind, I associated being adopted with being abandoned at birth. Even though I believed the story that my birth mother died, I still wondered about her. Was she young or old? Did she have other children? Could I possibly have a brother or sister? A twin? Since I wasn't getting any answers from my parents, I made some up. The stories I concocted never did involve a basket floating down a river like I'd learned about in Sunday school. I never pictured myself being left on someone's doorstop like on the evening news. I wrote my own scripts trying to make my birth interesting like the ones I saw on TV.

By the time I was born, my parents had been married fifteen years and were set in their ways. Mom, at thirty-seven years old, mostly fed me and sent me to my room to entertain myself. Dad, six years older than Mom, worked long hours and was tired when he got home. Unlike today's society, in which couples choose to have children later in life, mine were atypical. Everyone assumed they were my grandparents.

Although I'd like to say their age didn't matter to me, I know it did. Jealous of the other kids, I wanted what they had. Not just the right shoes or the cool clothes, their moms and dads were involved in their activities. My mom just dropped me off at the swim lessons and scout meetings that were coached by the other kids' moms and dads. Sitting cross-legged on the sidelines, hoping I wouldn't be the last one picked for a team, I couldn't help but notice how the coaches always selected their own kids as team leaders and presented their own children the top awards. I felt alone again, sitting on the curb, watching other families pile into their station wagons, waiting for my ride home.

I would have given anything for a brother or sister. To have someone to play with. Even someone to fight with. Anything would have been better than hanging out by myself, alone.

I could tell it was sunny outside by the gentle stream of light filtering through the slight split in the tightly closed wall-to-wall living room drapes. As the sound of laughter draws me toward the window, I place my book down on the sofa and walk toward the light, gently parting the curtains to sneak a peek of the outside world. Carefully making my way through the layer of heavy fabric, pushing aside the white sheers underneath, then separating a row of blinds, I feel like a prisoner catching a glimpse of freedom from inside her cell.

As I watch the neighborhood children playing in their yards, I wish I was with them, sharing in their fun. I am certain the laughter means they are truly happy. Seeing them chase the brightly colored balls, I keep hidden, making sure they don't notice me. As an errant ball rolls into our yard, I race back to the sofa, embarrassed, knowing the shrill order I heard: "Get off my property," came from our kitchen. How could I let anyone see me come out of that house?

Returning to my Nancy Drew mystery, I let my mind wander, imagining I'm the daughter of an international spy, or a rich recluse, kept inside, sheltered, for my protection. Even though I don't believe in fairy tales, I like to fantasize that a prince charming, on a white horse, will come to my rescue. This keeps my mind busy while I plan my escape. How I would run away. Although the thought is tempting, with no money for food, clothing or shelter, I know it is not realistic right away. But someday...

***

Although, technically, there was a lake in Lake Hiawatha, we summered at the Lake Hiawatha Country Club, where local residents swam in an Olympic sized pool rather than polluted lake water.

I sit cross-legged on my dad's old olive army blanket, wearing my nylon one-piece bathing suit with my oversized sweat shirt draped over my shoulders, eating my kosher salami on rye wrapped in butcher paper. I watch the other families emptying the contents of their Igloo coolers onto their colorful quilts. I envy their Baggies stuffed with bologna sandwiches on Wonder bread and lust after their Twinkies. I'm not allowed to have Twinkies or Wonder Bread. Dad says they are made with lard. We are kosher. Not the orthodox "no drinking milk with meat, two sets of dishes" kind of kosher that we learned about in Hebrew school. Our "kosher" is special. We don't eat pork. But shellfish is ok. Probably because Mom loves lobster.

I turn my back and pretend I don't notice the laughter from the bikini-clad blonde girls squealing with delight as their muscular, beer-logo, tee-shirt wearing dads swing them around like human carnival rides. I know not to disturb my dad as he sleeps on his green webbed aluminum lounge chair, plugged in to the Yankees game on his transistor radio. I don't need Mom, whose playing bridge with the "girls", to remind me, "Daddy works hard. Let him rest." Besides, I know, he wouldn't be able to lift me anyway. As the sky changes from blue to shades of pink and orange, and the card players' cigarettes burn down to their lipstick-stained filters, I stay on my blanket reading, wishing I fit in.

I have trouble concentrating on my book. My mind keeps wandering, trying to figure out why Mom and Dad adopted me since they don't want to play with me. If I only had a brother or a sister, I reasoned, everything would be different. I'd have someone to play with. Since I was more than enough trouble for Mom, I knew a sibling was not going to happen.

I thought of asking one of those other dads to swing me. Afraid they would say "no", I didn't. I just watched, secretly fantasizing that someday I'd marry a man who would swing my children around. I'd give my daughter a brother and my son a sister. I knew my children would have everything I never had. Their life would be better.

CHAPTER FOUR

Sylvia was one of those women you'd describe as handsome. Kennedy women handsome. Not dainty and glamorous like Jackie, Mom had an air of strength and power like Ethel Kennedy and Eunice Kennedy Shriver. She made her presence known. Tall, with big hair, big bones, she carried herself with grace and dignity. When dressed to the nines, her razor sharp wit and intelligence commanded attention. However, Mom was best known for her cooking. Her friends gathered at our home for the food. I wanted to cook like her.

I wish I had known my mother better. She didn't talk much about herself. As I watched her beat everyone at Trivial Pursuit and score the highest points in Scrabble, I always wondered why she never furthered her education. I assumed she wound up working at Bamberger's after high school because my grandparents couldn't afford to send her to college.

Mom wanted me to have a better life than she did. Not only did she expect me to excel in school, she wanted me to excel at everything. It was assumed that I would get straight A's, practice my piano three hours a day and dance like a prima ballerina.

From the tender age of three to the ripe old age of sixteen,

I studied tap, ballet and ended my run performing jazz. I loved dancing. I was a natural. There was only one thing preventing me from reaching my potential, going professional. Dancers are thin. Skinny. There is no place for a tush on a dancer. And rarely is a tutu designed for a support bra. I did have one thing going for me, however. I started out as the cute one. The littlest in the class. The one who didn't need to be a great dancer because the audience enjoyed watching me tug at my tutu while performing *On the Good Ship Lollipop*. Trust me; Shirley Temple had nothing to worry about.

Although my dad filmed my performance in the Caldwell, NJ, version of Swan Lake, in which I, as the star, was carried across stage by the school's director himself, my fondest memories were not recorded.

As a little girl, I used to look forward to my special time with Mom. After every dance class, while the other girls undoubtedly went home and burned off excess energy playing hopscotch and jumping rope with their friends, Mom and I would cross the street, hand-in-hand, to Grunnings coffee shop. There I sat swiveling in my seat behind the chrome topped counter, with my tutu and slippers safely stashed in my pink vinyl ballet case resting on the floor next to my foot, while Mom, fidgeting with her pack of cigarettes, waited for her cup of coffee to appear. I'd watch the boy behind the counter as he carefully stuffed chocolate ice cream all the way down to the bottom of my waffle cone. I couldn't take my eyes off my treat, observing how he carefully turned the overstuffed cone upside down, totally submerging it in a bowl of deep, dark, delicious chocolate jimmies until the creamy goodness virtually disappeared. After he handed my dessert to me, I'd immediately sink my teeth deep into the crunchy sprinkles, feeling like I was in heaven. I totally danced my heart out each week for this reward. And the best part, Mom never commented on how fast I ate or the way I lapped up the drippings before they slid too far down the cone as she daintily sipped her coffee, pinky finger pointed up in the air. I was happy.

She did her job. Taking me to piano lessons and ballet school, she put in the time. Only my mother wasn't merely providing me with a well-rounded childhood, or exercise, or a way to meet other children. She actually believed I'd become a professional pianist. Knowing a chubby dancer wouldn't get too far professionally, she eventually placed all her hopes for me into my piano future, never for a moment letting me forget how she sacrificed her beauty sleep getting up all those Saturday mornings to schlep me to lessons. My life took on a kind of pre-Julliard existence as Mom insisted I practice three hours a day, every day, after school. I played so much I almost believed her dream myself. For a while. Unfortunately, I peaked during Moonlight Sonata. It was downhill after that.

While Mom harped on the schlepping part of Saturday mornings, I focused on the performing part. After Mom would drop me off for my lessons, I had to stay and face "the music". My piano teacher, Mr. Bried, the man "who taught the famous Peter Nero", was the man who could make me a star. Since he was a stickler for classical music styling, hands stiff, fluent arpeggios up the wazoo, I constantly feared this little man, this Hunchback of Notre Dame clone, would yell at me and grade me poorly for slouching or for not playing with feeling. "You're so shy, so quiet," he scolded. Ready to cry, I gently wiped my nose with the tissue I kept in my skirt pocket to prevent dripping snot on his concert-sized Steinway. "There you have it! You can't even blow your nose with feeling!"

I wanted to get up and wring his scrawny little neck. No feeling! Do you want me to show you feeling? I wanted to say. Ask my mom if I have feeling. You should hear me at home. I'll show you feeling! But Mom wasn't back in the room yet to pick me up so she didn't hear this remark. She's always yelling at me for talking back, for screaming, for losing my temper. What would she say if she heard the man who, each week, is pocketing her hard earned dollars, say I have no feelings? No emotion? Would she stand up for me? Would she take my side? I didn't ask. I never told Mom what happened that day. I was afraid to tell her I planned to quit. Soon. Anyway, I didn't care for classical music. I wanted to play the songs I listened to on my radio. Sonny and Cher. The Temptations. The Four Tops. I wasn't interested in Bach, Beethoven, Rachmaninoff. Mom made me play his music, *for my own good*. I think one of her famous, "you'll thank me for this later" speeches followed.

I was so worried, scared, about my upcoming recital. What if I'm not good enough? What if I make a mistake or I play with no feeling? People will laugh at me. I'll be embarrassed. I prayed for the recital to be cancelled. Maybe my teacher could get sick. Just a little sick, I decided, making sure I was not asking God for him to die. I just wanted him to cancel this one recital. The night before I was scheduled to go onstage, Mom got a phone call. Mr. Bried was in the hospital. He had a heart attack. There would be no recital. I felt so guilty. I wished this on him. It was my fault. I was more powerful than I ever believed possible. That didn't matter. Nothing else was important other than I was saved from humiliation. I never went back to my lessons. Now, I figured, Mom could get back to her beauty sleep and I wouldn't have to practice hours and hours each day. Now I'd have the time to try out for twirling. I'd have a life. Or not. I started watching *Another World* after school.

From his thick Hungarian accent to the slicked-back, Fred Astaire hairline, Andre was what you'd call suave. Whether he was twirling Mom around the dance floor or serving snifters of Drambuie to guests in our formal, gold and black-flock wallpapered dining room, my dad was charming. Butcher by day, ladies' man by night, he was a class act.

Hanging out at his store on non-school days, I, more than anyone, knew how hard my dad worked. "Joanie Doll, it's time to get up," he'd whisper in my ear at five AM after he'd finished dressing. "Don't wake Mommy up," he'd remind me as he headed out to walk my dog Koko. When I finally dragged my half-asleep body into the bathroom to get ready, I'd hear Dad in the kitchen, preparing a thermos of coffee and bagging some bagels to take in the car. He wanted to hit the road by 5:30 since the butcher shop, in Irvington, was a long drive from home.

I was having a hard time getting used to riding shotgun ever since Dad traded in his gray, fifties style, clunker, "The Beast", for his new, refrigerated, delivery van. I preferred to ride in Mom's pre-seatbelt era, eight-cylinder, "Beauty". Her fancy, sky-blue Buick Electra, with its shiny chrome trim, had a hood so long it seemed as if we were miles away from the car in front of us. I felt safe. In Dad's new van with the words, "Andre's Meat Market, Free Delivery" painted in bold letters across the sides, there was no long hood for protection. The engine, housed in a large black box flanked by the two front seats, sat right between Dad and me. When he would stop at a red light, we were literally inches away from the vehicle in front of us. I didn't like that at all. I was scared, but I didn't say anything.

Leaving home in the pre-dawn darkness, Dad and I often marveled at a beautiful sunrise before making the one stop I dreaded. Like Alice falling down the rabbit-hole, entering the slaughterhouse was like plunging deep into an alternate world. However, instead of being excited about what lurked behind the door, I dreaded leaving the warmth of the van, knowing I would be standing for what would seem like an eternity next to my dad as he placed his order for the day. It was so very cold in there that I wore my winter coat, even in the summer.

Broken boxes littered the entryway to what seemed like the world's largest refrigerator. Unlike the one in our kitchen, with shelves for milk and special compartments for eggs and cheese, this walk-in refrigerator was lined with wall-to-wall animals, hanging on hooks like clothes at the dry cleaners. Unlike the prime rib or the porterhouse steaks wrapped in brown butcher paper that Mom cooks for dinner, this room was filled with meat that still looked like dead cows, only with no skin and no heads. And they were sliced in half. Ready for the picking.

As Dad walked through the room, I'd hold his hand, staring at the floor, trying not to step in the red liquid I imagined pooling by my feet. The blood. Luckily, I never witnessed the animals being killed so we would have food on our table. While

Dad talked to the men in the clean white coats, I continued staring at the ground, imagining those farm animals, cowering in the back, trying to hide. Secretly I hoped some would make a break. Escape their imminent death.

When I used to say "I'm a meat and potatoes girl just like Daddy," I didn't want to know where my dinner came from. I didn't want to think about those famous Jersey cows we pointed out on our weekend drives, grazing in the fields, each time I ate my dinner. I continued staring at my feet and watching where I walked as Dad pointed out "nice marbling" to the men writing up his order. Soon, back in the warm van, the cargo section loaded for the day, we'd drive in daylight to the store.

Andre's Meat Market was more like a little neighborhood grocery story. Its shelves were lined with canned vegetables, soups, salad dressings, even my favorite Heinz ketchup. Dad sold almost everything you could buy at Foodtown or ShopRite, there was just less variety. We ate our breakfast and lunch together in the back of the store, where the customers never went. After unlocking the front door, Dad would leave the "closed" sign in place until we were ready to open for the day. Leaving the lights off in the main area, we headed around the meat case to the back of the store, the storage, freezer area, out of customers view. I'd unzip my nylon hooded jacket and hang it on the low hook near the small bathroom with the leaky sink and rusty toilet. Dad would remove his tweed sports coat and hang it above mine. He'd then slip on a freshly pressed white apron and tie it in the back. I didn't need an apron since I "worked" with the customers, not behind the meat case. Never handling a large cleaver.

Before Dad would open the store for business in the morning, we'd pull two aluminum-framed, plastic covered chairs, up to the butcher's block that served as our dining table, where we'd eat breakfast before it was soaked with the blood from the sirloin steaks, the porterhouse steaks and even the pork chops, that Dad trimmed for the customers throughout the day. Dad would remind me that the pork chops were for his customers, not for us, since they were not kosher.

He'd lay out some white butcher paper as a table cloth, and let me choose the breakfast cereal I would have while he drank a cup of coffee and ate one of the bagels he brought from home. I wasn't interested in the cereal knowing there were Devil Dogs sitting on the shelf only a few feet away. Dad said I couldn't have any dessert until after lunch. Morning was so long as all I thought about were those Devil Dogs. I couldn't wait.

After our breakfast, Dad would go to the front of the store, turn on the lights, flip the sign to "open" and we were ready to start the day.

My favorite part of the day was waiting on the customers. Even though I couldn't see over the tall meat display case, Dad let me work the register on the lower counter to the right. We always knew the moment a customer entered the store. When the bell rang, Dad would stop whatever he was doing and dash to the meat counter, ready to make a sale. Proudly, he'd introduce me saying, "My daughter, Joanie, will be happy to help you today." Mostly I remember old ladies shopping. They were so happy to let me help them. I'd follow them around the store, placing whatever they pointed to in their basket, while Dad would cut their steaks or grind their hamburgers. When they were finished shopping, I'd total their order on an adding machine, the kind with rows and columns of numbers, and I'd open the cash register. Dad stood by my side, watching to make sure I gave everyone the correct amount of change. I sensed Dad smiling as his customers raved over what a bright daughter he had. Telling him, "You should be proud." I knew he was. Without Mom around, Dad never yelled at me. I could do no wrong.

Around midday, when there were no customers in the store, Dad would put the "out to lunch" sign on the door and we'd return to the butcher block table again. After wiping off the morning's blood, he again covered the butcher block with fresh paper. Still obsessing about that Devil Dog, I didn't even want to look at my sandwich. But before I had my treat, I not only had to finish my lunch, I needed to pass my drill. I needed to prove I knew all my times tables. Since Dad and I didn't have that much to talk about, he quizzed me in math. After answering all the questions right, I was finally rewarded with that damn Devil Dog. By this time I wanted more than one. "Math's important," Dad said. I knew the "you'll thank me for this someday", was implied.

After the last customer left the store, it was time to turn the door sign to "closed" and turn off the lights. Dad would tug off his blood soaked apron and toss it in the bin with the others waiting to be sent out to the cleaners. After washing up, Dad slipped on his tweed sports coat and we were done for the day.

While driving home, in the dark again like it had been that morning, I pictured Mom standing at the stove top, stirring her soup, worried that her chicken would be overcooked, dry, ruined. I hoped we were not in trouble for being late for dinner. I was tired after my long day. Too tired to fight with Mom, I'd make sure to keep my elbows off the table and try harder than usual not to spill my milk. Sitting at the table, I glanced sideways at Dad. I smiled at him silently asking, *Am I doing ok?* He understood my question, nodding back to me, with a wink.

***

The Friday after Thanksgiving, we headed out early for our semi-annual pilgrimage to the city. Dad, in his topcoat and Fedora, eased himself behind the wheel of Mom's Buick, pulled the car out of the two-car garage, backing it into the driveway. As he stepped out of the car to close the garage door, Mom and I walked down the front stairs of the house to the driveway. Mom opened the passenger door and stepped aside as I pushed the front seat forward to climb into the back of the car. Mom followed, carefully lowering herself into the front passenger seat so as not to mess her hair. As Dad adjusted his rear and side view mirrors, Mom pushed in the cigarette lighter and pulled out a white filtered Parliament from her purse. After rolling down her window, she lit the cigarette, inhaled deeply and nodded to Dad, time to go. As Dad pulled out of the driveway, I settled in for the ride, leaning against the side window, positioning myself for the best view while carefully avoiding the trail of Mom's cigarette smoke as she exhaled after each puff.

Navigating past the ranches and split levels, we passed a few remaining unheated log cabins, reminders of the old days when families, like my grandparents, left their homes in nearby Passaic to "summer" by the lake. Soon we approached the newer colonials, where the "wealthy" families lived. I heard Mom tell Dad some ladies at her beauty parlor were talking about buying their kids cars as soon as they passed their driver's test. She hoped I wouldn't expect a car. That didn't matter now. I was just happy to be leaving the house. Entering a world where no one knew me. The big city I see on TV. Continuing up the hill, approaching the main drag of Lake Hiawatha, North Beverwyck Rd, I imagined the scene through my car window as a Hollywood stage. As we traveled from the quaint set of *The Andy Griffith Show* to the Cleaver's more upscale neighborhood in *Leave it to Beaver*, I was looking forward to arriving in New York City, home of Lucy and Ricky.

Before long, traffic lights and advertising billboards replace dog walkers and bikers. Dad waits patiently for Mom to finish her cigarette and smash the butt into the ashtray so she can close her window and block out the street noise. Driving east on Route 46, Dad starts reading every billboard while Mom and I are on the lookout for the first signs of the city.

"There it is", I say, pointing a mittened hand toward the distance, where the foggy outline of the Empire State Building, the world's tallest skyscraper, peeks through the clouds. I'm anxious as I know it won't be long before I'll be holding my breath as we drive the seemingly endless one and a half mile stretch of the Lincoln Tunnel, fearing every stain on the grime coated walls threatens imminent death if the Hudson River chooses this day to come crashing down on me, us.

There's business to take care of before our date on Broadway. First stop, Mom's furrier. Dad and I sit and watch as Mom gets the royal treatment. Standing on a platform in front of the three-way mirror, Mom smiles as Dave, her furrier, appraises his work as if he were putting the finishing touches on a ball gown for Elizabeth Taylor. Determining no further adjustments are needed to her monogrammed, silk-lined, full-length mink, Dave nods, deeming his work perfect. Ready to show off her new look, Mom's old tweed coat is boxed up so she can continue her day in style.

Next up, the garment district. This time my dad poses elegantly in front of the three-way mirror as the tailor admires his handiwork on the stylish suede trimmed suit. After returning to our parking garage and carefully stowing Mom's old coat and Dad's new suit in the trunk, the three of us start walking to Broadway. Although, being Jewish, we don't decorate our house for Christmas, we do stop to admire each elaborate, holiday-themed, window display along 5th Avenue before stopping in the world famous FAO Schwartz to "just look at" the toys. After lunching at Sardi's we head out to the Shubert Theater, to enjoy our second row orchestra seats to see Jerry Orbach in the matinee performance of *Promises, Promises*.

Settling into my seat, my heart races as the lights dim and the orchestra begins warming up just a few rows in front of us. Soon the velvet curtains part and I dream that someday I'll be up there on stage. Someday I'll be a star.

Following dinner, still basking in the warm afterglow of my Shirley Temple, I hang on tightly to my parents' hands as we make our way down 44th Street, cross 5th Avenue to Rockefeller Center, where I skate under the world famous Christmas tree. Although our family outings didn't include throwing balls, or picnicking at the park, and I was never swung through the air like a carnival ride, at times, my childhood was magical.

***

The dashing figure hosting our famous Perlmutter parties bore no resemblance to that tired old man I watched shuffling to the dinner table night after night. Dressed to the nines, my dad's red-carpet greeting made company feel welcome. Long before Billy Crystal raved, "You look mahvelous," I witnessed my dad's, "You look ravishing," reduce dressed-up housewives to mush. As Dad bent deep at the waist, gently planting a kiss on a bejeweled wrist, I'd detect giggles coming from grown women. Noticing my father still holding that manicured hand as his lips wandered up her arm, I'd glance to the side, observing Mom's "look", telling Dad he'd gone far enough. Time to stop. Obviously this was all in fun since my parents had the best marriage in the world. If I knew anything for sure, when I grew up, I knew I wanted what they had.

Yes, Sylvia and Andre knew how to throw a party. And I got to help out. After Mom and I finished slaving in the kitchen and all the cooking was done, the hors d'oeuvres plated, wrapped in Saran Wrap and spread out on the kitchen counter, I got to sit on Mom's bed and watch her get ready for company. Leaning back on rows upon rows of throw pillows, I'd be careful not to get my shoes on the bedspread as I'd stare in awe, watching Mom select the perfect jewelry to go with her new, *make sure you hide the bill from Daddy when it comes in the mail*, dress.

Then I'd watch her meticulously apply her makeup, always aiming for Hollywood style glamour, never settling for the "natural look". Not even for grocery shopping. But this was party time so she added extra layers. So many layers I'd lose count. First there was foundation. Next came the loose powder. Then pressed powder. Finally the rouge, stroked liberally on her cheeks, gave her that "healthy glow" she said was so important.

Mom succeeded ingraining in me that I'm not dressed until my face is done. Blush, mascara and eyeliner were as much a part of her wardrobe as her 18-hour brassiere and rubber girdle. Finally adding "the piece de resistance", her red lipstick, she was ready to greet her guests.

Yes, I loved when Mom and Dad threw parties. While entertaining, Mom was always in a good mood. I could do no wrong. Whether throwing a birthday or a Passover Seder, Mom and Dad went all out insisting on nothing but the best for their guests. No Tupperware containers. No chips or dip. Mixed nuts were served in the Limoges china. Chopped liver went in the Lennox bowls. The Herend porcelain was for the main course. There were no exceptions to this rule, unless, of course, I wanted to polish the silver.

I always volunteered for kitchen duty. Whether it was portioning out the bowls of nuts or cleaning up after dinner, while Mom was busy with her guests I could taste as many goodies as I wanted, with no comments, no criticism. I didn't care if I got sick to my stomach.

It was more than the food that made party time special. Instead of being banished to my room, I was the star. The evening's entertainment. It was my job to show off those piano lessons that Mom schlepped me to every Saturday morning. Even after I quit taking lessons, I was paraded in front of the guests as if I'd just been accepted to Julliard. I loved my moment in the spotlight, feeling like a princess, watching Mom beam with pride as she coaxed me to center stage. If she wanted a show, I'd give her one. Pretending I was on that Broadway stage rather than in my living room, my heart raced as I approached the piano.

Standing next to my upright, positioned underneath an ornately framed Renoir, I felt just as special as if I were taking bows next to a Steinway at Carnegie hall. Mom, tapping her crystal glass with her silver knife, signaled it was time for everyone to gather in the living room. "I have asked Joanie to play the piano", she announced to the captive audience. With a cocktail in everyone's hand, the room quieted. All eyes were on me. Before settling onto my wooden bench housing music ranging from Bach to Beethoven, Broadway to Beatles, I'd dry my sweaty palms on my slacks and take a deep breath. Bending at the waist like I'd seen performers on The Ed Sullivan do each week, I'd offer a few excuses, "I haven't really had much time to practice this piece", just like Mom always did when serving her pot roast, "it would have been better but I ran out of..." Although never quite ready for my performance, I was thrilled to be asked. Mom, tapping her cigarette ashes into the crystal ashtray balanced in her lap, dismissed my excuses assuring everyone, "She's just modest." Turning to me Mom added, "Go ahead, Joanie. Show 'em what you've got. We're all waiting."

I'd get so excited. An audience. After a few stanzas of Fur Elise, the room would erupt in applause. For one moment, I was a star. I was loved. After playing a few more tunes from my repertoire, I'd take a bow and leave the piano, having done my job. Proof I was a good daughter, if not the best pianist.

As the guests filed into the dining room for dinner, the real musician, Mom's friend Ethel, remained behind, casually settling onto my piano bench and pounding enough red nail polish onto the white keys to ensure her signature boogie-woogie would be remembered for months, or years, to come. Knowing her natural talent was something I could only dream of, I was off to my next job. Serving the main course. I reveled in the oohs and aahs, as each guest drooled over the delicacies I helped Mom prepare. Once again, Sylvia made me the star declaring, "Joanie made that," even if I had only arranged the offering on its doily-covered platter. When we had company Mom lavished me with praise. I loved her party personality.

After dinner, Mom and I cleared the table while Ethel resumed her rightful position at the piano. As the men gravitated to the living room for after dinner cigars and cognac, I'd get to hang out with the women. Even though I didn't dare try one of their cigarettes or pour myself a real drink, I felt grown up as they treated me as if I were one of them, one of the girls. Someday, I too would be throwing parties just like Mom and Dad.

Late at night, lying in the quiet of my room, still on a high from my fun, grownup evening, I'd overhear parts of Mom and Dad's conversation in the kitchen, as they cleaned up together, reliving their fun party, looking forward to the next one. Yes. I would throw fabulous parties when I grow up. I resisted falling asleep, dreading the following day.

The morning after the party, with no cake to bake, no table to set or nuts to distribute, I was once relegated to my room. Yes, I knew my place. My room was where I belonged. And Mom's "go clean your room" was her not so subtle way of getting rid of me; letting me know who's the boss.

I had no idea who the real Andre and Sylvia were. Mom and Dad were almost as much of a mystery to me as the birth mother who gave me away. I should have asked more questions.

My dad was born in Hungary. I only remember him mentioning once, more as a footnote than a story, teary-eyed, that his mother and brother were killed by the Nazi's. End of subject. No talk of the concentration camps I'd learned about in school. Instead, when the war became a topic of dinner conversation, Dad dove into great detail about how he fought for our country in WWII, proudly showing off his war souvenirs, reminiscing how he and his buddies stole the swords off the Hogan's Heroes-like German soldiers after they passed out. He downplayed how hard he worked bringing his sisters and their families to this country. I knew he had two sisters. One was married and had a daughter. His other sister, thank God, had been liberated from a concentration camp. I knew not to question him about his family or the fact that the sister who survived the camps was married to a man who was not Jewish. I understood the subject was too painful. I knew not to ask.

We rarely saw Dad's side of the family. It could have been his choice, but I always got the feeling Mom didn't want them to be part of our lives. Again, I never asked.

Mom's family, my Grandma, Aunt, Uncle and two cousins, lived next door. Between Boy and Girl Scout adventures and trips to dude ranches and volunteering at the local ambulance squad, I knew my aunt and uncle were busy. Mom said I shouldn't bother them.

Dad, spending six days a week at the butcher shop, was tired when he got home. I shouldn't bother him. When he was home, he slept on the couch. I never quite figured out what Mom did all day when I was at school. Sometimes she worked. Not always. I wondered why she never went to college. She seemed so smart, and talented.

Once, I caught her playing the piano when she didn't know

I was nearby. Insisting I wasn't hearing music, she was merely cleaning the keys, Mom stopped the moment I entered the room. And those moldy, paint-peeled basement walls I passed on the way to the washer and dryer, displayed beautifully framed oil paintings, signed "SP". I never saw her paint. I never asked.

She read. Based on the number of library books regularly weighing down the mahogany coffee table, I assume Mom read a lot. I often wondered if she lived vicariously through those tomes, daydreaming about another life, the one she could have had, had she married money. Or perhaps she imagined the children she might have given birth to, had she married another man. A rich handsome man like Rock Hudson. Mom told me he was gay. I didn't believe her. Anyway, I'm sure she would have preferred a daughter who looked like her rather than the ungrateful brat she adopted. I knew she wasn't happy with me constantly rebelling and rejecting her authority. I'm not sorry for being opinionated.

Mom shopped and read. Perhaps she collected housekeeping tips or fashion advice from those *Family Circles* or the *Ladies Home Journals* neatly piled on the end tables. I'm sure she spent hours poring over the *Readers Digests* next to the toilet while I was at school, since this was the only time she enjoyed total privacy without me begging for my turn. Sometimes, I think, my mom just wanted to be left alone.

I liked when Mom had a job. When she was working, I'd get the kitchen to myself after school, until she got home. For a few hours I got to eat anything and everything I wanted. Sometimes I'd broil an entire chuck steak or finish a loaf of bread, one slice at a time, rolling each piece into a tiny dough ball before slam dunking it into my mouth. Often, I'd take a box of Hydrox cookies, fake Oreos that were made without lard, and stack them on the arm of my club chair. While watching *Another World*, I'd screw open all the cookies, scrape the cream filling out of each one, and put the filling together creating one huge cookie, hoping Mom wouldn't find crumbs on the floor. Sometimes I'd get lucky and find some candy hidden behind the good dishes in the dining room. By the time Mom got home I was usually so stuffed I couldn't eat another bite. I'd tell her she didn't have to worry about making dinner for me. She didn't ask me why.

Usually, after a few months on the new job, Mom stopped going to work and started collecting unemployment. I never knew if she had been fired or if she quit. She didn't say. I didn't ask.

Since Mom felt it was important to dress her best for every occasion, Mom's routine before leaving the house to collect unemployment was almost the same as her getting made up for a party. Like turning Robin Williams into Mrs. Doubtfire, Mom would apply her moisturizer, foundation and pancake first followed by the rouge, eye shadow and mascara. Finally, when her lipstick was on, and blotted, she'd study herself in the mirror and, if everything was in place, we were ready to go.

I wasn't sure what to think or where to look first time I went with Mom to collect unemployment. Staring at my black patent leather Mary Janes, I clung to my mom's side as she proudly stood in her high heeled pumps, sporting her favorite herringbone suit she probably bought off-season for 75% off Bloomingdale's suggested retail price. I can picture her leather pocketbook wedged tightly in the crook of her arm while we waited patiently to pick up her weekly check.

I'll never forget that smoke-filled room with its paint chipped walls and orange plastic chairs bolted to the floor. Many of the people in line wore Levi's and faded tee shirts emblazoned with team names like the one I wore at my summer day camp. Others donned skirts or slacks with crisp white shirts. Mom wouldn't let me sit down or touch anything. She said the seats were dirty. I wasn't allowed to make eye contact with anyone, but they stared at us. I felt different.

I sensed heads turn toward us when it was my mom's turn at the counter. I stared at my shoes as Mom politely answered the woman's questions. "Yes, I've been looking for work." I wasn't sure why I felt so uncomfortable at the time, although I knew I didn't want to go there again. After she received her check she explained to me that she had paid into the system and now it was time to get her money back.

With the check securely tucked away in her purse, we spent the rest of the afternoon at the Short Hills Mall. She shopped and treated me to ice cream. Before returning home Mom reminded me, "Don't tell your father what we bought. I'll hide the bill when it comes in the mail."

I knew very little about my mother other than when she wasn't throwing a party, she seemed unhappy. And it was my fault. I understood that our house would be happier if I would clean my room and show her respect.

I wished Mom understood how hard I tried to make her proud of me. Slaving over my homework. Studying all hours of the night to bring home A's on my report card. Practicing the piano three hours a day so I could perform at her parties. These things weren't easy for me.

All I asked in return was for her to leave my room alone. I never understood why I had to keep my room clean, neat, when I had a door. Why didn't she understand that by merely keeping my door shut we could pretend my room was clean? This made perfect sense to me. Why couldn't I make Mom understand that?

Since I spent so much time in my room when Mom was home, when she was away those few hours after I got home from school, I went nuts. Like that lab rat being let out of the cage into a maze, I was so excited to be free, I didn't know where to start, or stop. There was so much more to do than raid the kitchen.

When Mom was home, I followed her rule: walk, not run. Like I was living in a friggin' museum, I didn't need to be constantly reminded the house was not a playground. That china cabinet holding the Lennox bowls and crystal vases would actually rattle each time I passed through. I avoided the dining room, using the hallway whenever possible. Since I was so careful to walk slowly and quietly through the house when Mom was home, those few hours before she got home was another story.

"What are those spots on the ceiling?" Mom asked, her polished finger stabbing the air, not far from where I'm sitting watching TV.

Looking up to the ceiling, I played dumb, pretending I didn't know what she was talking about. "What?" I asked, not taking my eyes off the TV.

"I know it sounds crazy, but don't those spots look like fingerprints to you?" Mom was serious.

"Where?" I answered, actually making her point again to her "imagined" smudges. "Why would there be fingerprints on the ceiling?" I said, not adding, duh. That wouldn't be right.

I don't think she ever figured out that I practiced gymnastics on the sofa a few times. The cushioned back, about five inches wide, was pretty close in size to the balance beam at school. I used the wide, rounded, arm of the club chair for my "horse". Lightly touching the ceiling helped keep me from falling. I made a mental note to wash my hands better if I did it again. I thought about offering maybe the roof is leaking but decided to keep quiet.

I tried to cover my tracks, replacing the furniture I moved for my occasional gymnastics workout. So when Mom would yell about finding cookie crumbs on the carpet, I figured she was just looking for a crime she could prove.

Shortly after Dad sold Andre's Meat Market, I began dreading the moment he'd walk through the door after work. I guess Mom, no longer concerned about how tired he was in the evenings, began spending her afternoons accumulating and documenting evidence for my inevitable punishment. It was those times that I'd wished for a brother or sister the most, if for no other reason than to take the pressure off me.

I'm not sure if her list of accusations was written down or just in her head, but since my bedroom was right next to the kitchen, I'm confident Mom intended for me to hear, and understand, the details of each transgression she outlined to my father. Every act of disobedience that had triggered her tirade. Curled up on the floor hugging my knees, I'd stare at my reflection in my full-length door mirror. I'd watch how the tears filled my eyes before burning their way down my cheeks, finally reaching my lips. I'd test myself, trying to see how long I could put off wiping my face before licking away the salty wetness with my tongue. The room closed in on me as I'd sit still, listening carefully to each of her words, wanting to understand what she really thought of me. Ungrateful. Unappreciative. Smart-mouthed. I noticed how her accusations began slowly, gradually increasing in volume and intensity. Expecting her to crescendo soon, I quietly blew my nose, attempting to muffle my sobs. The last thing I needed to hear was Dad yelling, "Stop your crying or I'll give you something to cry about."

Eventually I got used to her tirades, almost feeling sorry for Dad having to be greeted this way, night after night. Why couldn't she just let him relax sometimes before inundating him with her increasingly creative fabrications, each one ending with, "Do something about your daughter. I can't take it anymore." When he'd enter my room, I'd notice his neck veins throbbing, the whites of his eyes red with blood. I almost felt sorry for him as he'd announce, "This hurts me more than it hurts you." Almost.

When I got too old for spankings, he'd just yell at me, never bothering to ask for my side of the story. I really wished I'd known what I did wrong. Could she really get that upset over my spilling a glass of milk? Maybe I ate something I wasn't supposed to. Perhaps I forgot to empty the dishwasher. Or was it just that I disagreed with her? Maybe that was what she meant by "disrespectful". I couldn't win. Who knows, she might as well have accused me of being responsible for the Cuban Missile Crisis. It's a good thing she didn't know about my gymnastics practice.

I liked when Dad just ordered me to stay in my room. It's where I wanted to be anyway. Where were those clever script writers when I needed them? The ones who gave those precocious kids on television and movies the perfect line that made their parents, and the audience, laugh? Or the writers who had Ward Cleaver say to the Beaver, "Tell me the truth and you won't get punished." That never happened in real life. I wish Dad would have asked me questions. Or at least given me the third degree, trying to get to the truth. Then I would have been able to present my side. That Mom was making things up.

I think what hurt the most was when Mom called me fat. I began sneaking a few of her Benson & Hedges to replace my afternoon binges, hoping they'd kill my appetite so I'd lose weight. At first the cigarettes just made me sick. I actually liked that. I got a little sympathy. Not much. Not enough.

In time, I began listening intently to the words she chose. The more I understood what she was saying, the more hurt I felt. "Fat and ugly". "Ungrateful and unlovable." She wasn't accusing me of doing something, like talking back to her. She was attacking me as a person. "She'll never have any friends," she'd tell my dad. Yes, I can understand her being upset with me ruining her chicken with ketchup, but does she hate me for being fat? Does she really think I'm ugly?

I didn't understand why Dad never listened to me when I told him she was making things up. Why he never took my side. It just seemed like after his long day at work, he had another job to do. I knew he couldn't enjoy his dinner or relax for the evening until he got Mom to settle down. The only way to do that was to take care of me. Then magically, as he left my room and entered the kitchen, the yelling would end.

In time, I stopped playing the role of victim. Learning to anticipate, and prepare myself for one of her tirades, I'd still assume my crouched position behind my mirrored bedroom door the moment she started. The difference was I began writing down those vicious words pouring through the walls as if I was in school taking notes for a test. I paid close attention to each word and its meaning, trying to make sense of what I was hearing. The more I listened, the less I cried. It was almost as if she was talking about someone else. As I carefully documented each of her accusations and criticisms, I'd make faces at myself, scrunching up my nose, sometimes pretending I was her secretary. "Did I get this right Mom? Did you say I'll never have any friends because I don't respect my mother? Or was it, I'll never have any friends because I'm so ugly? I really want to understand." I continued staring in the mirror, eventually putting down my notepad to fix my hair, try on makeup. Basically, I tried to stop caring. But I couldn't. I so badly wanted to read my notes back to her. "Mom, you did say fat, right? No one will love me because I'm so fat. Got it. "

Although Mom usually waited until my dad got home for "my lesson," she really didn't appreciate that time I taped and played back her thirty minute rant, naively hoping she'd understand how she hurt my feelings when she called me names. I'd lost count of how many times she kicked her foot into the wall before coming down on me with both fists. I was twelve at the time. I recall leaning against the wall and sinking down to the floor as I curled myself into a ball. I'd never seen her so angry before. I was scared. So many times I thought, *Mom's going to kill me...* I never before believed she'd really kill me, until now. Maybe that would be the best thing to happen. I couldn't live like this anymore, constantly being afraid of her. Always worrying I would say the wrong thing. Do the wrong thing. It seemed like nothing I did was right. I might as well be dead. But I was afraid of the pain. What if she had a knife in her hand? I tried to protect myself. I bent my arms at the elbows as I'd seen prize fighters do, to protect their face from being pummeled. "Please," I begged. "Just kill me now and get it over with." Suddenly, as if she'd been slapped in the face, Mom backed off. She never touched me again.

I so wished I'd had a brother or sister to take the pressure off me. Someone else she could take her anger out on. Or at least bear witness. It would have been nice to have someone on my side. Someone I could confide in. I had no one.

Looking back, I sometimes wonder if it was my fault I felt like a visitor in my own house. Like a foreign exchange student, temporarily living with strangers, I never got the feeling of "we". As in, "we" are a family. It was me against them. I disagreed with everything Mom said. She didn't understand me. If I complained about school, Mom sided with my teacher. So I stopped complaining.

I often wished my grandma lived with us instead of with my cousins. She loved me. With her blue hair and her round body, she was my sanity. When she'd come over I knew she was there to visit me. She'd ask me to do her nails. We'd play cards. She told me I was her favorite. She was my lifeline. But I couldn't, or wouldn't, tell her about Mom. How Mom was mean to me. I tried to handle that myself.

The more my mom pushed me away, the harder I tried to make her love me. Buttering her up in the kitchen, I'd rave over her cooking, begging her to tell me the secret to her fabulous cakes, her mouthwatering mandel bread, and her unbelievable chopped liver. She liked that. We had some good moments. Standing at our chrome-bordered Formica countertop, cupcake batter ready to go in the oven, I couldn't wait to tell Mom the new word I'd learned. "Guess what?" I said.

"Watch what you're doing," Mom said. "Don't spill chocolate on the counter. What?"

"I learned what 'fuck' means." I beamed. That was a big word for me.

"Oh, really?" She replied with no hint of surprise or anger, probably hiding a grin. She took this as matter-of-factly as if I had said, "I can name all the planets." "OK, what does it mean?"

"It means sexual intercourse."

"That's right." She answered.

That's one thing I admired about her. Although little things would set her off, when it came to those big events, potential life-shattering experiences, Mom was cool, calm and collected. While she would go off the deep end each time I clumsily dropped something onto her carpeted kitchen floor, she handled pressure well.

Walking through the front door and smelling smoke coming from the kitchen could not have been an enjoyable experience for Mom. And learning not to put lamb chops under the broiler before going to the bathroom was a valuable lesson for me. If you'd think having to call the fire department and remodel the kitchen due to my stupidity would have triggered an outbreak of rage, you'd be wrong. Mom was thrilled to have the insurance company buy her a new range and oven and I wasn't punished at all. Go figure.

And she barely raised an eyebrow when, during the height of the Vietnam War, I painted my bedroom black and hung "Make Love Not War" posters.

Was she calming down? Was she getting better? I wasn't sure. I loved being able to talk to Mom. I didn't want to press my luck.

About the time I learned the word *fuck*, I started learning more about sex and sexuality in general. When the girl who'd once asked me, "What was it like in the orphanage?" told me how a woman got pregnant, I went to Mom for confirmation. "Is it true?" I asked. "The man and woman get naked it bed, and, do it?"

"That's right," Mom said.

"Do they have to get naked?" I asked.

"Don't worry. You can keep your nightgown on," she said, smiling.

What a relief. When I told Mom that I'd never be able to have sex because I couldn't insert a Tampax, she didn't even laugh at me. She told me not to worry.

These are the times I like to remember. The times I felt close to Mom. When I could come to her with my questions, my problems, and she'd answer me, taking me seriously instead of making me feel stupid for asking. And then I'd go and blow it.

I guess I always knew in theory it took both a man and woman to make a baby, but I never thought about it in great detail. No one wants to think about their parents having sex. And since I was adopted, I figured whether they had sex or not had nothing to do with my being born. Suddenly, now that I was actually learning about the mechanics of sex, both at home and in school, where they're showing films detailing the process in which the sperm fertilizes the egg, I start to wonder about my birth mother again. Like when I had to make that family tree in grade school, I start thinking about my origins.

Since learning my birth mother died in childbirth, I already felt guilty that I killed her. Now I start thinking about the man that provided the sperm for my conception. What happened to him? I couldn't believe he died at the same time. That would have been too much of a coincidence. And men don't die in childbirth. I never asked Mom if she knew anything about my birth father. Maybe he was still around. I wanted to know if Mom knew anything she could tell me. That shouldn't upset her.

Standing at the kitchen counter getting ready to set the table for dinner, I made one more attempt to find out about my birth. This time I must have really hit a nerve. She had never before actually lost her temper at the birth mother question.

"You said my birth mother died in childbirth. What about my birth father? What happened to him? Do you know? Just because she died doesn't mean he died too."

"Don't ever ask me that again" she said, kicking her foot through the kitchen wall. Dropping the dishes I was holding into the sink, I ran out of the room. I knew her temper too well and I didn't like it. It took me this long to finally get it. She really didn't want me to know anything. I never asked again.

It's funny that so often I asked, "can you tell me anything about my birth mother," but I never asked about my own mother. The woman who was raising me. I never asked my mom "Why didn't you go to college?" "How did you meet Dad?"

I had questions. I had lots of questions. Most of them I was afraid to ask.

My most pressing question was, "Why do you hate me?" "What did I do?" She would have said, "You know what you did." Followed by, "Go to your room." Or, "Wait until your father gets home."

Just because I no longer asked about my birth, doesn't mean I didn't think about it. I continued studying other families in restaurants, at school events. I would look over at brothers and sisters fighting with each other. Then laughing. Teasing.

Playing games on the tic-tac-toe boards on the tables, having fun while the parents talked to each other. I made a point of noticing how everyone in the family looked similar. Strangers could tell they were related. I would notice how the boy and the girl would look similar, but not the same. At first glance he resembled his father. Maybe his hair was the same color. Then I'd notice he had his mother's nose. And the daughter would look like both parents as well. Perhaps she had her father's nose and her mother's hair. Who did I look like? I had a large forehead like my dad, but that didn't count. We're not even related. Not by blood anyway. I wondered, maybe my birth mother had other children before she died giving birth to me. Did anyone have my nose?

CHAPTER FIVE

I was the shy girl in high school. The quiet one. Keeping to myself, I sometimes thought my teachers didn't know I existed. I'd raise my hand to answer a question and watch them call on the other kids. Almost invisible, I'd wave my hand like Arnold Horshack on *Welcome Back Kotter*, frantically, hoping to show off my brilliance with the correct answer, only to be told: "Joan, we know you know the answer. Let others have a chance." When was my chance to shine?

I dreaded the nights Mom went to my parent teacher conferences. She'd come home questioning why all my teachers said I was quiet when I was always yelling at home. "Why don't you participate in class?" she'd ask me, never believing my answer that I raised my hand all the time and they rarely called on me. "Fine," I'd say, adding, "Why do you ask if you're not going to believe me?" Then I'd retreat to my room, slamming the door.

I hated high school. Rushing to the girl's room between classes, I'd glance sideways at Debbie or Bonnie or Cindy, some "popular girl", a cheerleading type, strutting down the hallway, smiling like she owned the world. *What the hell was she so happy about?* I wondered, figuring she was trying to decide which boy she'd choose for the prom and which one she would break up with. Maybe she was just planning tomorrow's outfit. I never smiled at school.

I couldn't wait until my classes were over each day. I just wanted to get home as soon as possible to raid the kitchen and watch *All My Children.* Living vicariously through characters such as Erica Kane, I dreamed of someday moving to New York and becoming a famous actress. That is, of course, if I lost twenty pounds. Actresses weren't fat. I needed the right image.

I was lonely. Sitting on my bed at night, deeply inhaling a Benson & Hedges from the pack I sneaked out of the carton Mom hid in the top drawer of the dining room breakfront, I heard noises, laughter, coming from behind the house. Balancing on my bed to peer out my small window, I noticed my cousins, partying. I could tell there were lots of other kids from our school in their back yard as well. I was careful, not wanting anyone to catch me watching. I'm sure they wouldn't mind if I joined them. But I wouldn't know what to say, or do.

One time my Grandma told me about those parties. She said the kids were smoking things they shouldn't. By the way she winked at me, I understood Grandma was talking about marijuana, the dangerous drug we learned about in our school assemblies. Grandma told me my aunt and uncle, the former Scout leaders, allowed the kids to smoke and drink in the back yard, rationalizing they were safer doing it at home. "You're a good girl," Grandma told me. "Don't think about them."

I tried not to. Grandma was the only one on my side. The only one who loved me. Even if I wanted to venture out, try a beer, find out what the kids were really smoking, I wouldn't want my grandma to be disappointed in me. I don't think she ever was.

Knowing I'd be home in the afternoon, I was the one Grandma called the day she had her heart attack. I was with her in the ambulance ride to the hospital. I got to say goodbye to her before they turned off her life support. I miss my Grandma.

I liked staying in my room. With the door closed, it was my

sanctuary. Enjoying free reign of the house before my mother got home from work, I made sure I ate enough to keep me from wanting dinner. I made sure to squirrel away everything I'd need for the night, knowing it was best for me to stay away from the kitchen after Mom got home. Hoping to lose weight, I mostly stashed diet food. Melba Toast. Apples. Cheese wedges. I counted on the cigarettes to kill my appetite. Lessen my hunger pangs. I remained in my room until it was time for school the next morning, only sneaking out to go to the bathroom.

After my grandma died, I inherited her B&W portable TV. Now, I didn't even have to leave my room to watch *That Girl* or *Gidget*, two of my favorites. When there was nothing on, I'd read. *Love Story, The Chosen, Portnoy's Complaint, Valley of the Dolls*. Stories about neurotic, sexually frustrated, drug addicted Jews seemed to be my favorites. The real world. Although not planning on using drugs, or enjoying random sex with strangers at glamorous parties, I figured reading about it was a lot safer than going out there and experimenting. I didn't want to be one of "those girls" everyone whispered about, or worse, one who had to suddenly drop out of school. Reading about them, however, was exciting, and safe.

I wished my life was different. I wished I were different. More outgoing. I wanted to belong. To be invited to a party or a prom. To be out there with people. Doing, instead of reading, watching. But I didn't know how. I didn't know what to say to people. Sometimes I wondered if Mom was right. Maybe I was too ugly, or fat, for people to like me. Then I realized there were many girls at school who were much fatter than me. Even the fat ones smiled in the hallways. Had boyfriends. Went to dances. To proms. It must be me, I thought. I must be doing something wrong.

My cigarette diet was working. Finally down twenty pounds, I was feeling great about myself. I agreed to go to a youth group dance. This time, instead of playing wallflower, standing alone in the corner, a boy asked me to dance with him. After the music ended, he didn't just walk away as usual. He asked me out for a date. A real date. One where he would pick me up at my house. In his car. We'd go out to a movie. Maybe have dinner first, or ice cream after. I was excited. Maybe my life was turning around. It's the diet, I thought. Now I was attractive.

I guess I was naïve to think that he actually liked me when he asked me out. Instead of the fun, Gidget-like evening like I expected, he just brought me back to his house, telling me his parents were out of town. Then he wanted to show me his room. I didn't want to see his room. I wanted to have fun. Maybe it was my fault. I didn't really ask what he had in mind for our date.

Yes, I followed him up to his room, expecting to receive the whole "twenty-five cent tour" of the house like my parents gave when they invited a new couple over to a party. I didn't really want to see his living room, dining room, kitchen, or bedroom. I wanted a real date. Something I could talk about. Write about in the diary that I would start now that I had a real life. No, he just wanted to show me his bedroom.

He started kissing me. Holding me tightly and kissing me on my mouth. Wasn't the kiss supposed to come after the date? Then he started tugging at my zipper. Reaching back to shove his hand away, I knew something was wrong. I felt really uncomfortable, but I didn't know what to say. What to do. I pulled back, and he pulled me closer, easing me down on his bed. It took a while, but I finally got through to him that I wasn't interested. I didn't want to sleep with him. He took me home.

For some reason, I still hoped he liked me. I hoped that his kissing me meant he was very attracted to me and that he would want to try again. This time do it right. Like in my favorite books, he would come to his senses and realize that I was worth waiting for. That my refusing to have sex with him was a sign of integrity. Quality. Something he'd want in a girlfriend.

I was wrong. After days of waiting, sitting by the phone willing it to ring, I realized he was never going to call me again. I felt humiliated. I guessed my mother was right. Even though I lost the weight, I was still unlovable. There was no hope for me.

Staring in the bathroom mirror, I couldn't decide which would be a better way to end my life, to stop my pain: swallowing a bottle of aspirins, or making a nice, neat, slit in my arm with one of the razors I use to shave my legs. I analyzed my choices. Aspirins are pills, like in *Valley of the Dolls*. I could just take some, a lot, with water, then go back to my room, read a little while and fall asleep, never to wake again. It could be a full day before anyone would wonder what happened to me since Mom doesn't even get up in the morning when I leave for school.

I tipped the Bayer bottle, spilling a dozen or so white tablets into my cupped hand. Then I remembered my aunt telling me that people who really want to kill themselves slit their wrist lengthwise, up the arm, not horizontally, like they usually show on TV. Since she was on the ambulance squad, I figured she would know. Maybe the razor would be the way to go. Feeling the coolness of the shaver's metal handle in my hand, I rationalized; I could bleed into the sink, and wash the blood down the drain. That would be less messy. I didn't want Mom mad at me after I was dead for messing up her bathroom. And the razor would be quicker than waiting for some pills to take effect.

I start getting dizzy, feeling faint. I need to sit. I pour the aspirins back into the bottle, and place the bottle down on the pink marbled vanity. I lay the razor blade, still in the shaver, next to the bottle. I lower the carpet-covered toilet seat down and sit, resting my head on my lap. After taking a deep breath, I lift my head and stare at the black and white herringbone-patterned floor tile. As my eyes lose focus, I watch as the tiles seem to float, creating designs. I try to picture tiny animals, mice, hamsters, scurrying across the floor like I do when staring at the clouds. I notice the dull murmuring of the TV in the room next to me. Mom and Dad are still awake. They will need to use the bathroom soon. This is not a good time for...

What am I doing? I get up and go back to the sink. I stare at my face again. It's now splotchy, and hot. I fill the sink with cold water and soak a washcloth in it. I wring it out and lay it on my face. *Am I thinking about ending my life because of a boy? No.* I argue with myself. *I can't stand living with my mother. I can't stand being me.* Snapping out of it, I ask myself, *What if it gets better? Things could pick up and I'd never know if I didn't stick around to find out.* I hear banging on the wall. "Are you ok?" Mom yells. "You've been in there a long time."

"I'm fine," I scream back. I am, now.

I put the aspirin bottle back in the medicine cabinet. I return the razor to its plastic holder and place it in the vanity drawer. I clean up the bathroom, returning the toilet seat to its full upright position. I decide, the hell with it, I'm going to start living my own life. Do whatever I want. I need to start living. To make a life for myself. No more feeling sorry for myself. No more pitying myself. As soon as I get my license. Once I can drive, there'll be no stopping me.

In the meantime, I decide to accept my life as it is. To sit back and become an observer. I analyze the characters in my TV shows. Patty Duke has an identical cousin that she never knew about. I start fantasizing about my birth family. Who knows? Maybe I have a cousin, or even a twin. The *Brady Bunch* kids all had hair of gold, like their mother. I wonder if I have someone's hair. Maybe someone else out there cannot wear bangs. Someone curses at their cowlick every day. There is a "Joanie" on *Eight is Enough* and on *Happy Days*. Where would I fit in these families?

I always wanted a big brother, like my cousin has. If I had a big brother I'd have someone I could play with. Talk to at night. Confide in. Hang out with. He'd be my witness when Mom would yell at me. Maybe he'd even stick up for me. Maybe he'd take the blame. Maybe his eating habits would irritate Mom more than mine did. If I had a brother I could meet his friends. Maybe date his friends. That was my problem, I realized. The other girls had brothers and sisters. They had built-in friends. That's why I was alone. Someday I will create my own family with a brother and sister. I'll have a daughter who will have a big brother. The best big brother in the world. That is my plan. A definite plan.

CHAPTER SIX

After graduating from high school, I needed to get away. My best friend Nicky and I hit the road, heading up to her hometown in Montreal. I was getting bolder. Asking for permission didn't get me anywhere. I learned to tell Mom my plans, without waiting for a response.

I started out small. "Nicky and I are going shopping," I announced one day in my senior year.

"Who's Nicky?"

"My new friend," I told her, unceremoniously reaching for Mom's matches on the kitchen table to light my Kools.

"How come I never heard of "this Nicky" before?" Mom asked.

"She just moved here from Canada."

"Why don't you invite her over for dinner sometime?"

Invite her for dinner was Mom's way of learning more about someone. Giving her the opportunity to subject my new friend to the third degree was the last thing I wanted.

"Sure Mom. That would be great."

Nicky was cool. Not only did she have a boyfriend, he was a cop. Not only was her boyfriend a cop, he was a black cop. Yes, she was cool. I only met her boyfriend once. He came into the diner where Nicky got me a job. He seemed nice but I knew Mom wouldn't think so. I'm sure Mom wouldn't even have approved of Nicky since she wasn't Jewish. So when Nicky asked if I wanted to drive up to Canada with her in her new car, I didn't hesitate. "Yes."

When Nicky picked me up for work at 7:30 for our night shift, I called to Mom on my way out the door, "I'm leaving for Canada tomorrow. Bye." I didn't give her time to argue.

After one week in Canada, with my new taste of freedom, I was more than ready to go away to college. Although I didn't have a clue what I'd do with my life, I knew I needed to continue my education. Being the only child of Jewish immigrants, I understood my job was to be a doctor, or marry a doctor. I failed miserably.

College would be a different world. Feeling like an outsider for most of high school, I looked forward to a chance for a fresh start. Where no one knows I never went to the football games or the prom. This would be my opportunity to start my real life. To reinvent myself. Or perhaps, invent myself for the first time. I chose the University of Pittsburgh.

Why Pittsburgh? Not because it offered a quality education or for its great sports reputation. I chose Pitt because the brochure said it had a high male to female ratio. I wanted a boyfriend. And Pittsburgh was close enough to New Jersey to go home to visit occasionally, but far enough away to be totally on my own. Mom and Dad agreed to my choice because they had friends who lived there.

It was late August. I was still seventeen. The day arrived when it was time to leave for the airport, and not a moment too soon. There weren't any teary farewells. I hugged my parents at the gate, boarded the plane and buckled up. I looked forward to the full breakfast our travel agent promised. Those were the days. My first flight ever, from Newark to Pittsburgh, turned out to be a piece of cake. Getting a taxi to take me to the campus was easier than I had expected, especially since that cute pre-med student sitting next to me on the flight offered to carry my bags and share a ride to school. Everything was going smoothly until I reached the campus and realized that I left my wallet in the taxi. Thank God those friends of my parents lived close enough to lend me fifty dollars. Although I was not off to a great start, I forged ahead with determination. With my map in hand I dropped my luggage off in my dorm room and headed to the building where the freshman orientation was to be held.

The huge auditorium was packed to capacity. Despite the heat, the crowded room filled with excitement as if the freshman students anticipated a rock star would materialize at any moment. The room suddenly quieted as everyone noticed the lone bearded man in the tan corduroy jacket standing at the podium, patiently waiting for their attention. This is it. This is the moment I'd been waiting for. I'm in college now. I took a deep breath to calm my nerves, counting on this being the beginning of my new life.

I listened intently to the speaker's words, trying to ignore the fact that, without my wallet, the only possessions I had were my student ID card and the money I borrowed. Although the speech was long and boring, to this day I've never forgotten this one comment the speaker made. "Everyone look at the person seated next to you. One of you won't be here next year." Nervous laughter filled the room. I feigned confidence. With a big smile, I placed my neighboring students on notice. I was here to stay. Or so I thought.

College was so cool. Better than I ever dreamed it would be. It was so different than high school where everyone felt imprisoned in the building from 7:37 AM to 3:45 PM every day, having to get permission to go to the bathroom! I enjoyed the freedom of being able to set my own schedule. With some classes in the morning, some in the afternoon and some in the evening I was free to come and go at will. I could study at the library; hang out at the student union; or practice (hustle) pool, my new hobby. I just couldn't bear going back to my dorm room. Having spent so many nights alone in my room; that was the last place I wanted to be now.

As I checked out the political groups and observed protests of the Vietnam War, I began emerging from my cocoon. Perhaps too fast.

That pre-med student invited me to my first frat party. I had never tasted beer before. Although I didn't like the beer, that other stuff they were drinking wasn't too bad. The mixture of Tang and grain alcohol relaxed me and made me giggly. By the end of the first week I decided my morning class, French 101, at 8:00 AM, was not working out that well since I couldn't wake up before 11:00. I learned how to drop a class before it would show up on my transcript. No problem. It was as if I'd never enrolled. I didn't need French anyway. What a waste of time, I thought.

About three weeks into my freshman term, again unable to force myself to return to my empty dorm room, I hadn't realized it was almost morning as I sat curled up with a book in the Towers lobby. In walks, I should say, in stumbles, my destiny. With his long, blond, cocker spaniel curls, I couldn't resist his boyish charm. Sitting down on the bench next to me, he told me he just left a party and was looking for another one. I just happened to know a pre-med student I could visit any time. We stayed up in that room for an hour or so. He told me he lived far away, and asked if he could spend the rest of the night in my room. I said yes. He passed out on the floor. I lay in bed, watching him sleeping so peacefully, like he had not a care in the world.

After Ryan awoke, we talked for hours. I didn't want our time together to end. But he was a student. He did need to attend classes. And so did I. That afternoon he left me to return to his apartment, high on the hill. I didn't know if I'd ever see him again. That same evening, without even calling, he returned to my dorm. He rarely left my side again.

My favorite class was philosophy. And not just because it was at 2:00 in the afternoon, a much more reasonable time for those of us with a social life. I hate to admit I liked this course because the students were allowed to smoke in class. The desks had built-in ashtrays! I didn't have to sneak around anymore, flushing evidence down the toilet. I didn't have to walk Koko to smoke. Not being at home, I didn't have to answer to anyone but myself. At school it was not only cool to smoke, but your choice of cigarette showed how cool you really were. You've come a long way baby, one TV ad touted. I sure had. Enjoying my Kools in class relaxed me and helped me come out of my shell. It felt good. During my first week of Philosophy 101 I studied Nietzsche and Sartre. In my second week I learned that I'd get an "A" if I attended classes, or a "B" if I never showed up at all. I opted for plan "B".

I never missed my favorite Psych 101 classes until I wound up in the hospital. The health center couldn't figure out why my neck was so swollen. A cold? The flu? They weren't sure. "Drink plenty of fluids and try to rest," the nurse advised. I stayed in bed and got my classmates to take notes for me while I guzzled chicken soup and downed ice cream. My throat began to hurt worse than ever. When my head felt like a knife was stabbing my brain through my ears Ryan insisted I go to the emergency room. They admitted me immediately. "You have mono," the doctor informed me, looking over at my unkempt boyfriend, with a stern look on his face. I had the feeling I wasn't the first student to succumb to this ailment. "It's bad." He said. "Possible liver damage. We need to call your parents."

That was the last thing I needed. This was the first time I was on my own and within a month I had screwed up royally. Not only had I dropped classes but I wound up in the hospital. How would I explain this? Needless to say my parents were not too pleased with my stay in the hospital or with Ryan, in his fringed suede jacket, standing by my side, plying me with ice cream. In their minds my being sick, and dropping out of classes, *was his fault*. And they would have been partially right. I was not used to a social life. I wanted to hang out. I enjoyed going to the cool parties. Sleeping was a waste of time. I never wanted to go back to my dorm. That was too depressing. Besides, Ryan had alienated my roommate the first day he met Ruthie asking her, "Are you wearing a Halloween costume?" referring to her bright orange top. She wasn't, of course. No, I couldn't go back to my room.

If Ryan and I weren't at someone else's dorm, we were at his place, watching the mushrooms grow in the bathroom. Not magical mushrooms. Just your typical mushrooms that grow in dark, damp environments. Disgusting. But I didn't care. I wasn't home. I wasn't alone. For once, I felt like one of the cool kids. I was having fun.

Eventually, my new lifestyle stopped being fun. While listening to *Highway to Heaven* for the thousandth time, I realized I was not enjoying watching my new fiancé bogarting the joint his friends passed around. Since I only liked him when he was straight, I asked him to stop smoking. He didn't. However, he promised he would stop when we got married. I believed him. I wanted to believe him.

Since leaving the hospital I had trouble going back to classes. Still tired from the mono, I could barely sit up, no less trudge through the snow to get to the other side of campus. Once again, I found myself confined to my room. Studying from classmates' notes was not the same as attending lectures. I passed the first semester, barely. I was still determined I would not be the one to drop out. I would not be the one who would not make it through the year.

I tried. Armed with a new attitude after returning from Christmas break, I planned to be the best student on campus. No more late nights. No more partying on weekdays. No more of that nasty Tang and grain alcohol concoction that the kids drank in the dorm. I would study, sleep and go to classes. That was the plan until I got the flu in my second week of my second semester. Feeling like a failure, I dropped out.

After being on my own for almost a year, I couldn't go back home. I couldn't go back to my mother's house. Since my dorm room was paid for the rest of the semester anyway, I stayed at school. I tried to tell my mother Ryan and I planned to live together for a while, before getting married, but she wouldn't hear of it. So, to make her happy, we set a wedding date: his graduation day. In two weeks.

Whenever my phone rang, I worried it was Mom again, asking why we were in such a hurry to get married. She wouldn't listen to me insist I just wanted to live with him. She didn't think that was proper. We'd be living in sin. I never even told her I had dropped out of school because I was sick all the time. She didn't know Ryan would sneak me back food from the cafeteria since we couldn't cook in the dorm. She didn't know how he took care of me. She didn't care that he loved me. And I couldn't tell Mom that, even though I couldn't afford to live on my own, coming home was not an option. In my mind, since I couldn't support myself, moving in with Ryan was my only option. I didn't have a choice.

Of all the things I couldn't tell my mom, I sure as hell didn't want her to know I was worried about Ryan's drinking and drug use. It was the seventies for God's sake. The era of sex, drugs and rock 'n roll. I rationalized, that's what kids do in college. They experiment. They get away with the things their parents wouldn't allow them to do at home. Then they grow up. He was the normal one, not me, being afraid to experiment. I'm too uptight. I convinced myself I didn't have anything to worry about. Did I? So why worry Mom for no reason? He loved me, and I loved him. That's what counts. The marriage would work out. It had to.

I came home from school a few days before my wedding. Having just turned eighteen, Mom, still concerned about me getting married, tried to get me to change my mind. "You are way too young," she told me. When that didn't work she added, "You are both from different backgrounds. Different religions." Her arguments fell on deaf ears.

"He loves me," was my only defense. Not only did a college senior like me, he loved me enough to want to marry me. Mom had said no one would ever even like me. My nose was too big. I was selfish. But he liked me. Ryan wanted to be with me all the time. I wouldn't tell Mom about how I didn't like when he drank or smoked. The only thing that mattered was he loved me. I liked that. Ryan listened to me complain about how Mom treated me, telling me I'd never have to worry about her anymore. I liked that too.

Defeated, Mom decided she'd get involved in the wedding plans.

Sitting at the familiar wood grained Formica kitchen table, coffee cups in hand, Mom and I, discussed (argued about) my upcoming wedding. Although I hadn't been away from home very long, the room felt different now. As I stared at the brick pattern wallpaper and matching brick-look carpeting, I noticed how the paint was starting to peel off the yellow cabinets. In the background, I waited for the cornflower blue Corning Ware coffee pot to bring the water to a boil on Mom's new Sears Kenmore cook top. Mom pulls the string to open a new pack of Benson & Hedges while I chain smoke my Salem Lights. The Entenmanns's Cheese Danish is ready to serve in the middle of the table.

"You're not getting married in jeans." Mom insists. "What will everyone say?"

"Fine. We won't get married. I didn't want this wedding in the first place. Remember? I told you, we were just going to move in together for a while."

"You can't do that." Mom argues. "What will…?"

"I know, what will everyone say? Why do you give a damn about what everyone else has to say? It's none of their business."

"I gave gifts to all my friends' children when they got married. You're getting married. End of conversation."

"I'm wearing jeans." I argue back.

"This conversation is not over."

I noticed the tulips were in full bloom on the day of my wedding. I felt beautiful in my white, empire waist maxi dress. It didn't bother me that everyone asked if I was pregnant. It felt cozy getting married in our living room. I was happy my whole family came for my wedding. The Aunt, Uncle and cousins that live next door were there. Even Dad's sisters, the ones I barely knew, showed up for the occasion.

A few of Ryan's relatives were there, as well as a group of his college buddies. While his parents sat quietly in a corner, most likely observing how Jews behaved in their natural habitat, his friends entertained my parent's guests with beer drinking contests and light bulb eating exhibitions. I just wanted to get the day over with. Since I'd left home, I no longer felt I belonged, if I ever really did. My black bedroom walls, already covered with faux wood paneling, were ready to become the backdrop for Mom's new TV room. I felt displaced.

Ryan, however, seemed so happy. Being the proverbial fish out of water didn't seem to faze him in the least as he, following my lead, went around the room hugging everyone. Even the caterer. He liked how my family seemed warm, unlike his mother, who kept her distance, remaining in the background. He enjoyed the party, the love, and mostly, the free-flowing beer. Dad always kept at least one six-pack in the house for gentiles, figuring that's what gentiles drank. For this occasion, he stocked up.

My friend Nicky was my bridesmaid. She stood up for me even though she thought I was making a mistake marrying a man who drank too much and smoked pot. I shouldn't have confided in her. She didn't believe that he'd quit. I did.

As I listened to my parents' judge friend asking, "Do you take...?" I noticed my dad's face as he stood to the side, dressed in his signature bowtie and custom made suit. I saw tears fill his reddened hazel eyes. "Don't ever forget you're Jewish", he said to me as he passed my hand to my new husband. I never forgot.

I truly believed that, when we got married, things would be different. The excess drinking, pot smoking, would be a thing of the past. A moment in time. What college students do. Like some girls having random sex at frat parties, waking up in strange rooms, not knowing the name of the boy asleep next to them. Or that special Tang I drank. It's a school thing. A rite of passage. What we do when we are away from home for the first time. The mistakes we make, our choices, don't necessarily define us for life. Ryan graduated with an engineering degree. That's respectable. No, that's admirable. OK, just because he barely made it to his last classes doesn't mean anything. He graduated. He put in his time. So he had fun his last year. He sowed his wild oats. That's a good thing. Now it should be out of his system.

I had it all planned out. I figured after graduation Ryan

would secure a fabulous, high paying job. Knowing he'd have to get up for work, not school, each day, would make him a responsible citizen. He'd wear a suit and tie, maybe even a white or light blue IBM-ish button down oxford, and I'd be waiting for him at home, preparing a great meal for my hard-working husband. If he wanted a beer, or a martini after a hard day, why not? On weekends we'd throw dinner parties, go to movies, and watch TV, all those normal day to day activities grown-ups do. Married couples don't hang out partying all hours of the night. After college, Ryan would be a responsible citizen.

The honeymoon phase of our marriage didn't last very long after I found a Baggie on our wedding night. Flushing the contents down the toilet, I wanted a divorce right then and there. What stopped me was Mom's voice in my head saying "I told you so". I wanted my parents to believe my marriage was perfect. I wanted them to think I made the right choice. Getting married at eighteen was not a mistake. I convinced myself I could make it work. Why should I doubt that? He promised me that was the last time. He just had some "stuff" left over from school. I believed my husband. Besides, he'd already landed a great new job that he'd be starting when we got back home. Everything would work out. I was sure.

We only lived in New Jersey for a few months before Ryan got a job transfer to Pittsburgh. We moved into a cute little apartment and soon purchased a brand new townhouse with three bedrooms. A master bedroom for us. A guest room for my parents. And an empty room that would be a nursery. Everything was going well. I got a temporary clerking job during the day to earn extra money, planning to go back to school for my degree after I had children. I studied photography at night. However, what I wanted most was to have a baby. My plan was to get pregnant the moment I turned twenty one.

By the time I was twenty-one, while most "new adults" are hanging out in bars enjoying their first legal drink, I was already a homeowner with a thirty year mortgage and an Irish setter we named Rusty. And we made friends. I got to entertain like my parents did. Only instead of formal dinners with music, our neighbors come over to watch the Super Bowl. It was fun. The men were even nice enough to carry my husband upstairs to bed after he passed out from too much liquor. After that night, I emptied the house of all alcohol. I didn't worry. I was confident Ryan would be fine as long as he wasn't tempted.

I was ready to start a family. The timing couldn't have been better. It's about time something went my way.

Not long after the *Pittsburgh Press* proclaimed: "Record Unemployment", my manager called me into his corner office. I assumed he wanted me to feel special as he sat me down and told me, "You're not being fired. You have been chosen as the employee we need to lay off."

"Why me?" I asked, surprised. I hadn't seen this coming at all.

"Mary complained you make faces at her."

How could I defend myself against this accusation? I was being let go because, apparently, I have no control what my face does. To make matters worse, this was the one day Ryan drove me to work because my car was in the shop. This was the day I had to stand outside, coffee mug in hand, waiting for a ride. I was humiliated. But I had plans.

Determined to have a baby, I decided this was the perfect opportunity to toss out my birth control and get busy. Losing my job was a good thing, I rationalized. My unemployment checks would carry me through the entire pregnancy.

Success didn't take long. In just a few weeks, with no period, I ran to the doctor. There were no home pregnancy tests at the time. I just knew I was successful. I was right. That night Ryan and I celebrated. I had ice cream and I allowed him one glass of wine. That little amount shouldn't hurt. Besides, he deserved it. I hadn't caught him with anything suspicious in months.

The very next day after the doctor confirmed my pregnancy I found myself sitting on the toilet, doubled over in pain. As I wrapped my arms tightly around my waist, I prayed I wouldn't find blood. Holding a fistful of toilet paper close to my body, my hand trembled as I bit my lip, willing myself not to look at what I knew I would find. I failed. It was worse than I imagined. There was not only blood, but a large clot, the size and color of an over dyed Easter egg. My heart raced. I felt dizzy. I didn't know what to do with what looked something like the placenta picture in the biology book I'd been studying to imagine what my baby looked like each day.

I didn't know if I should wrap it up and take it to the doctor or save it in a box. As my hopes and dreams fell from my trembling hand into the toilet, my options disappeared. Ryan took it in stride, not having a clue how I felt.

When my doctor confirmed the miscarriage, I felt alone. Empty. Guilty. I knew I shouldn't have rearranged the furniture the day before. This was my fault. This was all I wanted in my life. I wanted to be a mother. I wanted a family. I wanted my chance to have the life I'd always dreamed of. I didn't give a damn that the doctor said I should wait a few months to try again. Stopping at the drugstore on my way home, I bought a special basal thermometer, determined to not miss out on my next opportunity.

Mom knew something was wrong when she heard my voice over the phone on a Wednesday, rather than my usual Saturday call. Since moving out of the house, our fights were becoming few and far between. I didn't tell her about my husband's drinking, and she didn't ask. I gave her this opportunity to step up to the plate. She could hear my voice tremble as I said, "I lost the baby."

"At least you know you can get pregnant. You'll have lots of children."

Mom hit a home run.

About three weeks after my miscarriage I got tired of feeling sorry for myself. I took Rusty out for a long walk before driving to Baskin Robbins for a well-deserved mint chocolate chip cone. When I got home I called for directions to the unemployment office and made plans for my first visit. It seems that twenty years later, I'm following in Mom's footsteps as I find myself in another unemployment line. The smoke-filled room with paint-chipped walls and orange plastic chairs bolted to the floor feels too familiar. Again, I feel out of place. Even wearing jeans like the others, somehow I don't belong. With my college, ok one semester, education, I should be managing a store, not standing in line, asking for a handout. But right now this is for the best, I tell myself, as I beg the nice woman in front of me to hold my place in line while I run to the ladies room to vomit, wondering if it was the fish I'd had for dinner or the thought of the taxidermist I passed along the way. I knew this visit would not end at an ice cream parlor.

The next day, while fitting me for my first pair of contact lenses, my eye doctor steps back while I unceremoniously pass out in his chair. Surrounded by all the machinery for fitting glasses, I find myself awakening to the smell of ammonia, just like the women in the fainting scene of a period movie. Where am I? What's going on? "Don't worry," my eye doctor assures me. "Some of my most successful contact lens wearers pass out their first time. Maybe you're hungry."

Leaving the eye doctor's office, I find a deli in the mall. After polishing off my pastrami on rye, with extra pickles, I can't help but think the vomiting and the fainting were more than a coincidence. I couldn't be pregnant, could I? I'd been trying ever since my miscarriage. But I got my period. Although the bleeding was light, I marked it off on my chart and started graphing my next month. I did wonder why my temperature still hadn't dropped like the book says it should. My brain was spinning. I wanted to be pretty sure before I ran to the doctor to get the official verdict. At home that night, obsessing again about making another doctor's appointment as I dipped my kosher dill pickle into ketchup, I started worrying what the doctor would say if I wasn't pregnant. What if he thinks I'm crazy? Or worse, what if he says, "Relax, it'll happen." Doctors always belittle my concerns.

Another week of vomiting passes before I finally make that doctor's appointment to find out what is wrong with me. I'm thrilled to hear, for the second time, the rabbit died! This time the doctor questions me more thoroughly. "Tell me about your medical history," he asks. "Did your mother ever miscarry?"

"I don't have a medical history," I repeat. "I'm adopted."

By the time my pregnancy is confirmed, I'm pretty much vomiting all day, every day. Since I gave up smoking when I started trying to get pregnant, I need to find another way to calm down my stomach. Discovering a Baskin-Robbins close to home, I realize a pint of mint chocolate chip is a good, temporary, fix. And often my trip to the ice cream parlor is my only outing of the day. Every day.

It's a good thing I am able to get unemployment checks through the mail because I no longer have the strength to stand in line, or even walk the dog, for that matter. And, not taking any chances, I definitely don't plan on risking another miscarriage by moving furniture or pushing a heavy vacuum cleaner around the house.

Shortly after getting my exciting news my mom called, telling me Dad was in the hospital. He'd had a heart attack. I threw an overnight bag in my car and drove on autopilot the six and a half hours to New Jersey, heading directly to the hospital to visit him. Mom and I, holding hands, stood in silence as Dad lay motionless. Under starched white sheets, with clear tubes going into and coming out of his veins, he was barely recognizable. I stared, counting the steady rhythm of the saline drip as the fluid traveled down one tube to the needle imbedded in his pale arm, while averting my eyes from his catheter. The flashing lights on the monitor reassured us he was still alive.

Since I'd moved away, I always count on Dad shouting, "Joanie Doll", when I enter a room or call on the phone. He said nothing. Lying so still, I doubted he was aware of my presence. I wanted to talk to him, tell him how much I loved him, tell him to hang on, but I knew he needed his rest. He had to get better. I could give him something to live for. I leaned down close to his bed and whispered in his ear, "You're going to be a grandpa! I'm having a baby."

On our next visit home, during my second trimester, Ryan and I didn't mind that our pregnancy took a back seat to Dad's new toy. Removing his shirt, we enjoyed watching Dad demonstrate how his pacemaker, which looked just like he had a pack of my mom's cigarettes stuck in his chest, was not only keeping him alive, but how he was able to hook it up to the telephone and check to make sure it was working properly. I was thrilled he was doing so well.

My third trimester, other than still vomiting once in a while, went better than I'd expected. Ryan, being as supportive as he could be when he was home, entertained me for hours on end letting me win at gin rummy and scrabble. He even cooked a few meals on the evenings I didn't have the strength to get up. I kept up with my doctors' appointments, and enjoyed shopping for baby clothes and wallpaper, anticipating the blessed event.

All went according to plan, until the shit hit the fan. When Ryan is out of town on business, I can't fall asleep at night until he calls, letting me know he is all right. Exhausted from not sleeping well, when the phone finally rang at eight in the morning, I shifted my eight-month girth in bed to reach for it. Panicked, I didn't know whether I should wait for a logical explanation or start screaming at him right away telling him how worried I was.

I didn't catch everything he said. Bar fight. Knifepoint. Gave away his company car. What the hell was he doing in a bar? I didn't know what to say. I held the phone in one hand while I cradled my swollen belly in the other. *Where else would he be?* I thought. *Why did I expect anything different? Why would I not expect him to go to a bar when he's away on a business trip?* But his boss didn't expect this behavior. He had no idea about Ryan's drinking. He gave away his car? "What the hell is going on?" I finally asked.

At eight and a half months pregnant, with my husband fired from his job and interviewing for a new one, I found myself coaching Ryan on how to spin the fact that he's ready to relocate now, having already quit his job. There I was, the good wife supporting my husband no matter what, "standing by my man", sucking it up, needing to give him another chance. This time, not for the sake of our marriage, but because our first baby was due in a few weeks. Smiling through the pain, I put on a good show for my parents so they wouldn't find out the truth. I couldn't bear to hear "I told you so". More than that, I had to keep my act together to help Ryan find a new job. Once again, in crisis management mode, I worked to mitigate the damages.

Within a week, our freshly wallpapered townhouse was on the market, sold and we were on the road, moving away from Pittsburgh, and back to my parents' house in New Jersey. The last place in the world I expected, or wanted to be.

Mom put on a good performance, pretending she was happy we were living in her house. Having had almost four hundred miles between us had done wonders for our relationship; I didn't want to ruin the progress we'd made. She liked her time alone, so I stayed out of the way, busying myself trying to find a new ob-gyn and contacting realtors in Virginia, where we'd be moving for Ryan's new job, as soon as the baby was born.

It was my birthday, and Mom invited over the girls for dinner. Her girlfriends. I wished I could find my friend Nicky, but since I'd moved away, we'd lost touch. And her phone number wasn't working anymore.

After spending the day shopping for a new wardrobe for Ryan's new job, I found myself catapulted back to the old days. There we were again, sitting at the same dining room table where I had celebrated every holiday growing up. Same gold-flocked wallpaper. Nothing had changed, except me. Surrounded by their cups of coffee, cigarettes and Entenmanns' chocolate fudge cake, Mom and her girlfriends, Estelle, Bea and Ethel, flanked me, watching as I held my belly and checked my watch..

I was no longer a little girl feeling grown up, as I had been years ago when they let me join in their party. Now I was the one at the head of the table, nine months pregnant and ready to pop. I glanced over at each of these women, noticing how we had changed over the years. As a child, I considered Estelle the beautiful one. With her blond hair and elegant, manicured nails, I always thought she was so stylish. I was surprised when Mom confided in me that she "did her own hair", as if not going to the beauty parlor was a crime, or a sign of lower class. I hated going to the beauty parlor. Was that Mom's subtle way of telling me again I should have my hair done?

Bea, Mom's younger friend, was married to Dad's cousin Rudy. Mom said she "was a saint for putting up with him." I always liked Rudy, however. Aside from his loud personality and his stinky cigars, he was the only one who brought me chocolate Easter eggs for Passover. And he introduced me to Galliano. He seemed very loving to his wife as he held her cane and helped her up the stairs since their car accident.

And Ethel, the pianist. Her hair was as black as ever, but it was her signature red nail polish that caught my eye. The same polish that left permanent marks on the white keys of my piano. I wish I could play like her. Maybe my baby will play the piano.

Until this moment, it had never occurred to me that none of these women had ever given birth. As I tried to explain that I was feeling funny, about every five minutes, they all agreed with Mom when she said, "Don't worry. You're not due for a few days." I knew better.

I awoke at two in the morning, feeling a tightness, unlike anything I'd experienced before. I woke Ryan and called the doctor. Leaving a message for the service, I laid back in bed waiting for the phone to ring. Within moments, all the phones in the house rang. Even though I picked it up immediately, my dad was already on the bedroom extension. "Dad, please hang up." I told him. "It's for me."

My new doctor, who I hadn't even met yet, was on the line. "How far apart are your contractions?" He asked.

"About 5-10 minutes, I think."

"Call me back when your water breaks," he told me.

As long as I was up, I went back to the bathroom. After splashing some water on my face, I sat on the toilet. My water broke. I said to Ryan, "If you're going to take a shower, do it now. We're leaving for the hospital as soon as I'm dressed."

Living in Pittsburgh, I'd made plans with my doctor to have a natural childbirth. Against drugs, I was determined to give my baby the best start in life. I was going to do it right. Upon arriving at St. Clare's hospital in Denville, the same hospital where my dad was treated for his heart attack, reality hit me, fast. Lying in bed waiting for the doctor to arrive, my labor set in with a vengeance. Unlike that ridiculous movie I saw on natural childbirth, with the music and singing and dancing, and everyone, including her other children staring at the woman's vagina, I was not content to lie there, breathing and focusing on the stupid picture I brought. I was dying. My pain was on my spine. This kid wanted out, and was headed in the wrong direction. At that moment I decided natural childbirth was bullshit. Why should Ryan get to use drugs while I deny myself? If there ever was a time for drugs, this is it! "I'm going to die," I yell to the nurse. "Give me drugs."

The Demerol worked great. When I came to I was propped up in bed being told to push. I pushed. And pushed.

As they whisked away my baby boy, I barely got a chance to see his face. They assured me that he was healthy and that I would see him soon, when I got back to my room.

Without his mask, I didn't realize the man who walked into my room was the doctor who had just delivered my baby. "How are you feeling?" He asked.

"How's my baby? When am I going to see him?"

"Another doctor will be in to see you shortly," this stranger told me.

My mind was spinning. All alone in the room, I didn't know where Ryan was and why they weren't letting me see my baby. What the hell is going on?

"Is something wrong?" I asked.

"Your baby has a club foot. A specialist will be in to talk to you soon."

My heart stopped, as my mind pictured Dustin Hoffman's Ratso Rizzo from *Midnight Cowboy*, with his twisted leg, begging for handouts. I wanted to curl up and die. Moments later, in walks a nurse with the most beautiful baby boy cradled in her arms. As she hands me my son, my tears drip onto his perfect face as I lean in to kiss him for the first time.

Within minutes, a pediatric orthopedic surgeon enters my room, assuring me that he has already started treatment and that by the time my son is in school, we'll never know anything was wrong. He gently lifts the blue blanket covering little Brandon revealing a full leg cast, already in place.

All alone, my newborn in a cast, Mom at home "cleaning the house" preparing for our arrival, I'm wondering where my husband is. By dinner time, I'm getting frantic with worry. He doesn't even know about the club foot yet, or the jaundice that will keep both of us hospitalized for an entire week. I came in with a baby and I wasn't leaving without my baby, I thought while staring, alone, into the isolette, where my tiny bundle, with the cast and eye goggles for protection, is being treated.

"You made your bed," Dad tells me on the phone, explaining how he bailed Ryan out of jail. He didn't need to say any more. Dad didn't know the half of it. Giving away his company car. Getting fired from his job. Now with a baby, I have more reason to stay with my husband. To support him. To cure him. I have no choice. I just pray this time he's learned his lesson. Maybe this is the bottom they always talk about. He had promised he'd quit drinking after we had a baby. I wanted to believe him. Now I need to believe him. What choice do I have? Maybe this was his last time. Maybe he saw the baby's foot during the birth. He knew something was wrong before I did. Maybe he was self-medicating, traumatized by the fact that our perfect little baby, wasn't born as perfect as he'd hoped. Maybe Ryan couldn't take the pressure. Maybe he was worried. He never talked to me about it.

Except for the time each day when they let me insert my hands into the attached gloves of the isolette, pretending I'm touching my newborn's skin, I remained in my hospital room, my arms empty, my breasts swollen. Without my baby, I felt more alone than ever.

After a full week in the hospital, armed with a case of pre-filled formula bottles and instructions on how to bathe an infant in a cast, Ryan picked us up in his brand new red Buick Regal company car and drove our little family to my parent's house. After dropping us off, it wasn't long before my husband packed for his trip to Virginia, and headed out the door, determined to find us a new house so he could start his new job, in just two short weeks.

Maybe it was best that he left for a few days. As they say, out of sight, out of mind. The last thing I needed was to spend my first few days home from the hospital fighting about his arrest. Or, should I say his drinking? His broken promises? Dad was right. I made my bed. I need to deal with it. Later. Right now, excuses are the last thing I need to hear.

Worn out after months of vomiting, the firing, selling the house, helping him find a new job, giving birth in New Jersey, pretending the bailout never happened and moving to Virginia, I finally relax as I watch my baby, fast asleep, for the first time, in his new crib. He's the miracle I've been waiting for my whole life. This baby is part of me. My blood. My family. Between feedings and diaper changes, I took pictures. I couldn't take my eyes off his face. Perfection. When I wasn't staring at his face, I stared at his pictures. I compared his pictures to my baby pictures. Yes, he looked just like me at that age. My dream had come true. Finally, someone looked like me.

I was not done making my family. I didn't need a doctor to confirm my next pregnancy. It had been only three months since Brandon was born, so I just refilled my prenatal vitamin prescription and set up an appointment around the time I expected to hear the heartbeat.

My children were born twelve months apart. I was more interested in seeing if my baby's feet were perfect before learning if I'd had a boy or a girl. *Thank you, God.* My perfect daughter has an older brother. My prayers had been answered. I had the perfect family. And we were happy. Brandon and Katie had friends in Virginia. I joined Jazzercise. We moved from a townhouse to a house. Ryan worked out of a home office, allowing me the freedom to go grocery shopping when the babies napped.

It wasn't Ryan's fault when he lost his job during the winter of 1980. The company was cutting back on their sales staff and his position was eliminated. Once again we had to put our house on the market. With skyrocketing interest rates, we were lucky we had an assumable mortgage. After selling our house in one week, we were ready to go.

In no time at all, Ryan landed on his feet again, securing an even better managerial position in Ohio. We were ready to move and start our new life.

Fulfilling my wedding day promise to my dad, as soon as we moved to Ohio, I enrolled Brandon and Katie in a Jewish preschool. After that, they attended Hebrew School on Sundays. When Ryan was not out of town traveling for his job, he enjoyed assisting the coach of Brandon's little league. I proudly attended every game, cheering my son on as he batted the ball out of the park. Or tried to. He was very good at this sport. But my emotions went deeper than mere pride. Watching my son run the bases, knowing that his first two years were spent in a cast, brought tears to my eyes. I felt I was witnessing a miracle. His doctor was right. Other than the tiny scar on Brandon's Achilles tendon, no one would ever know he was born with a deformity.

And Katie. My ball girl. Sporting the same little purple and white uniform as her brother, my daughter was having the time of her life. Our house was always packed with their friends, running from room to room. Having fun. I did good. My prayers were definitely answered. Although, I still worried about my dad.

Knowing the severity of his heart disease, I made sure Dad got to spend quite a bit of time with his grandchildren before he passed away in 1983, at only seventy-two years of age. Every holiday, we'd come home, and I'd watch the joy in his face showing Brandon and Katie off in temple. As I sat next to my dad, watching his hands grip the prayer book he read from every day of my life, I noticed, for the first time, the frail curve of his shoulders, wrapped in his yellowed tallis. His salt and pepper curls peeking out from under his black yarmulke. Through my dad's eyes, I understood the meaning of the Yiddish word, kvell. To be proud of, to have pride; often with regard to one's own children. This was far more than the pride Mom felt watching me play the piano. Dad's pride involved just knowing my children existed. His love had no bounds. I did good.

It was after Rosh Hashanah. There was no more company in the house. Ryan, Brandon and Katie were sound asleep in their makeshift beds in the guest room. Mom had stormed out of the house after throwing a fit at the way I didn't defend her for trying to teach my kids correct table manners, or something like that. I was never sure what set her off. I accidentally knocked one of Mom's sconces off the wall and Dad and I were sitting together in the TV room, Elmer's glue in hand, trying to repair the damage, praying she won't find another thing to blow up at. After Dad reassured me he'd keep this secret, I finally got up the courage to ask the question that has been on my mind as long as I can remember.

I put down the glue, looked directly into Dad's hazel eyes, and asked, "Why does she hate me?" He remained quiet. I continued. "Sometimes, when I was growing up, I felt that maybe if the two of you were divorced, and she just had me, then she'd love me."

He looked away from me as he responded, "Your mommy loves you."

That was the last time I ever spoke with my dad. He died before my next regularly scheduled Saturday phone call.
The funeral, following orthodox law, was scheduled for the following day. I threw clothes in a suitcase for our trip to New Jersey. Ryan, Katie and I picked Brandon up directly from school. I drove the distance since Ryan's restricted license only allowed him "to and from work" privileges.

At the funeral, I silently said the Shema, the prayer Dad and

I said together nightly after he would tuck me into bed. *Shema Yisrael*... "Hear O Israel, the Lord our God, the Lord is One."

Mom and I, holding hands, watched as the funeral home filled to capacity. Being a fixture at the temple for years, countless congregants attended, showing their respect. Many friends and relatives, most of whom I hadn't seen since childhood, offered their condolences. Brandon and Katie, sitting still like little angels, would have made their grandpa proud. I prayed Ryan didn't drink any of the Manischewitz. That was the last thing I needed to deal with.

Although it was difficult leaving Mom alone in New Jersey, she insisted she was ok. We headed home, back to a life that would be forever changed.

CHAPTER SEVEN

As my dad so aptly put it, I made my bed… Living with an alcoholic was not easy. If I thought I was lonely as a teenager that was nothing compared to the shame of hiding everything about my existence.

After one of the dads on Brandon's little league, the one who owned a bar, made the comment, "I've never seen anyone drink that much before in my life," about my husband, I got serious, insisting there would be no more alcohol brought into our house. Despite my demands, I found bottles. Night after night, I lay in bed, listening to Ryan's even, rhythmic breathing, willing myself to keep from sneaking out of bed and searching through the pockets of all his pants, suits, even his golf bag, hoping, praying I wouldn't find evidence of …of what? Even though I wasn't sure what I was looking for I always found something. Pot, assorted loose pills, receipts. Behind cabinets, in drawers, under car seats. Everywhere I looked, I always found some evidence that told me Ryan had broken his promise to me.

Even when I'd hold the empty bottle up to my face as if I was selling Listerine on a TV commercial, he denied my accusation, claiming, "That bottle must have been there for months." That bar receipt I waived in his face, dated less than a week ago? Denial. He wasn't there drinking. "That bar has the best hamburgers anywhere," he'd insist. His next line would be, "How dare you deny me a good hamburger!"

I don't know who was in more denial, him or me? Did he actually believe the lies he told me? As he stared directly into my eyes, never looking away or turning his head to the side like they say liars tend to do, I wanted to believe him. I couldn't. Not anymore. But I couldn't leave. Having two young children counting on their father's paycheck to pay the mortgage, keep a roof over their heads and food on their table, I couldn't give up. And I couldn't complain to Mom. She'd remind me she'd told me so. Or she'd tell me to come home. Honestly, I don't know which choice was worse.

I tried to make friends with Brandon and Katie's friends' parents. However, as soon as they realized how much Ryan drank, they stopped answering my phone calls. They refused our invitations.

I wondered what happened to that boy who loved me so much. The one who stayed up night after night with me, planning our future. Was I that wrong about him? I can't give up.

Brandon and Katie were in bed. I told Ryan I was going out shopping. I lied. I hesitated before walking into my first Al-Anon meeting. In the back room of a church, the chipped, well-worn folding tables were butted together, lined up along the far wall. I took a seat in between two women who looked like anyone I'd find at a PTA meeting. It was fifteen minutes before the scheduled starting time listed in our weekly newspaper. A woman at the end of the table ruffled some papers together, possibly preparing to speak. I kept quiet.

"Welcome to Al-Anon", one of the women said to me. "Do you have an alcoholic in the family?"

I'd never talked to anyone about that before. I guess everyone is here for the same reason. I'm in the right place.

Why did it take me so long to come to a meeting?

"Yes, I do." I answered. "My husband."

"You're in the right place." She smiled at me, encouraging me to continue talking.

"I'm so worried that he'll lose his job. And our car insurance payments are so high, we can't afford them. I need to help him stop drinking." I expected this nice stranger to pat me on the hand and tell me, "Don't worry, everything will be ok." She didn't.

She obviously didn't understand as she replied, "Al-Anon is not about fixing the alcoholic. It's about fixing us." I looked at her. What does she have to worry about? Sitting there in her pressed jeans, her fancy sweater, her nails polished to perfection, I was sure she didn't need to worry about paying her bills. I got up and walked out the door convinced no one understands what it's like to live day to day worried if your husband will get fired. Worried if he'll get arrested. I need him to get better.

I went home determined to fix him myself. Since the "if you love me you'd quit" speech didn't work, we tried counseling. When the "board certified" counselor suggested I stop nagging and go out with my husband to enjoy a nice glass of wine, at a bar, I needed to find an alternate plan. What would that be?

If all else fails, threaten. I decided we'd moved enough. New Jersey to Pittsburgh. Pittsburgh, back to New Jersey. New Jersey to Virginia. Now, in Ohio, I'd come to the decision I can't uproot myself each and every time Ryan changes jobs. Now that Brandon and Katie are in school all day, its time I go back to school and get my degree. If I ever plan to make it on my own, I need a degree. In the winter of 1984, enrolled at Cleveland State University, I verbalize my threat: "Clean up your act by my graduation, or I'm getting a divorce. You have four years."

Mom was so proud when I told her I returned to college. In the short time since my dad passed away we had begun a totally different relationship. Sometimes I wondered if she had been jealous of how close Dad and I were at times. How we both enjoyed the same food and watched ball games together. Sometimes strangers would even remark how much I looked like my dad, not knowing I was adopted. Mom and I would laugh, but I could tell it bothered her. No one ever said I looked like my mom. Maybe that was why she wanted me to frost my hair. To look more like her.

Now that Dad's gone, Mom has nothing to be jealous about. Or maybe she just realized I was all she had left. Her childless friends had no one after their spouses died. Without me, she couldn't see her grandchildren. I don't know what brought on her change, but I was thrilled we were getting along so well. But I still couldn't confide in her. My marital problems were mine. I had to deal with them by myself.

Earning my college degree was like getting a second chance in life. My last chance to get it right. To stand on my own two feet. To be able to support my kids financially, on my own, if a divorce is necessary. I decide I will not let Ryan, no matter what he does, no matter how much trouble he gets into, stand in my way of an education. I will stay married until I graduate and he will pay for it. And why not? He was the reason I dropped out in the first place. He owes me this much.

Ryan knew my goal. He knew my timeframe. All he needed to do was clean up his act, get clean and sober by the time I graduated, or I'd get a divorce. End of story. Almost.

Then Mom got sick. In all my years of marriage, I worked hard to keep Mom from knowing about Ryan's drinking and smoking. I'm not sure who I was protecting, him or me. If I told her the truth, if I faced reality, I'd be forced to make a decision. Or at least give a plausible explanation why I would stay in such a marriage. No matter how bad the situation got, I kept everything to myself.

In a nutshell, there were a few DUI's. Then his driver's license was taken away. After Ryan "tried" something on a business trip, he wound up in the hospital, followed by his first stint in rehab. In order to be released from rehab, he was coerced into attending AA meetings.

Ryan agreed to go to AA meetings, under one condition.

That I go with him. Week after week I grew encouraged hearing so many success stories. How men and women reached their bottom, and climbed on the sobriety wagon, their lives changed for the better. I had hope. I figured Ryan must have reached his bottom by now.

Moving from state to state, each time he was fired, must have helped him realize drinking was bad. Giving away the company car, being held at knifepoint, was worse than most of the bottoms I heard in our nightly meetings. I could never understand how he always landed on his feet. I seemed to be the one who suffered, not him. I'll never forget at nine months pregnant, being delivered by a doctor I'd never met. When will I laugh at how this addict, while I was on the delivery room table about to give birth to Katie, when I was fully dilated and in pain, asked me if I was really sure I wanted to spend $100 on an epidural. "No," I should have said. "Why don't you use the money to go out and celebrate?" Again, I'm trying to figure out why I stayed so long in this marriage.

I found it very convenient that there was an Al-Anon meeting right next to each of the AA meetings. Since nothing else has worked, I started dropping Ryan off at his AA meetings and decided to give Al-Anon another try. It couldn't hurt to check it out. If nothing else this might be the one place I could talk about my secret life. Hiding bottles. Flushing the contents of Baggies down the toilet. Hiding money. Would the well-dressed men and women in this room be shocked? Or would they understand, be supportive? Do I need to keep on bearing this shame alone?

This time I didn't say anything at the meeting. I sat. I listened. I heard success stories that were different than the AA stories. These success stories didn't involve fixing their alcoholic. They didn't involve finding the right treatment hoping their spouse or parent would stop drinking. Would keep their job. Would be a better parent. The Al-Anon members related stories about how *they* were improving. How *they* slept at night, no longer going through their husband's pants pockets looking for receipts like I do. How they stopped flushing bottles down the drain like I do. How they spend time playing with their children, rather than sitting by the window waiting for their husband to come home.

Sitting in that meeting, I recalled how, as a child, Mom and I would fix dinner and wait. And wait. And wait for dad to come home. I'd watch Mom, staring out the window. Now, years later, I spend half of my life, staring out *my* window. Waiting for *my* husband to come home. Always waiting, praying, worrying. I wasn't living. I wasn't being fair to my children.

Brandon and Katie heard what was going on. They heard the yelling. The fights. They didn't know their dad was supposed to be home at six for dinner when he'd show up at three AM They heard me yelling at him. I was the bad guy. I didn't tell them what was going on. But they knew something was wrong.

"Daddy has a disease," I finally said, on our way to their first Alateen meeting.

I wanted to be fixed after one or two Al-Anon meetings. I soon discovered it didn't work that way. First I needed to learn to "Let Go Let God." I needed to learn that my looking for trouble didn't help the situation. I would find out what I need to know in due time. In God's time. Not mine. "Keep coming back," they told me.

I did. Three or four times a week, we recited the Serenity Prayer:

"God, grant me the serenity to accept the things I cannot change,

The courage to change the things I can,

And the wisdom to know the difference."

Afterwards, I hung out at Bob Evans with my new group of friends. I was thrilled to have friends! I loved Al-Anon. They understand me. These people know my secrets and they still like me.

Looking back now, I wonder how I made it through college. After Ryan lost another job, he started his own business. He was lucky enough to secure a major contract, guaranteeing us income for an entire year. The catch was he needed to continue working. That turned out to be problematic. After his latest relapse, he wound up in rehab and needed my help to run the business.

There I was, maintaining a full course load by day, running to the courthouse to get plans and specs in between my classes and sneaking engineering drawings into the treatment facility by night. At home I was afraid to answer the phone dreading explaining to suppliers and end users why Ryan could never be reached to address their questions. I was exhausted. And I still needed to feed and take care of Brandon and Katie.

I wondered when my life would get better. Sitting in the halfway house visiting Ryan, I was all but ready to give up. The stale cigarette smoke hung in the air like the fog rolling in under the golden gate bridge. The man in the corner rests his hand rolled cigarette in the gap between his front teeth. Another man is sleeping in the corner. Most are oblivious to the TV set in the corner of the room playing my video tape of Dustin Hoffman in *Rain Man*. I'm actually the only one watching the movie as Ryan is busy poring over the blueprint I brought him. I am anxious. We need to win this bid to make our next mortgage payment. It's important he doesn't get caught working. That's against the rules.

I wanted to be a good mother. I always tried to be home by four to greet Brandon and Katie with a plate of home baked cookies, before I dragged them to some godforsaken place to visit their dad.

As I dealt with the bed I made, always assuring Mom everything was fine, she did the same with me. I had no idea she was in such pain. She never said a word. Was this going on for weeks, months? Who knows how long? I never knew she was sick. So when she said her "flu-like symptoms" weren't going away, I worried, insisting she see her doctor. She didn't want to bother a certified medical professional. Instead, she visited her friend Ralph, a retired doctor.

Dear Joanie,

I'm feeling a lot better – thank God! Thought I was doomed to spend my life in the famous tiled room!

Spoke to Ralph about my condition (sought a second opinion!) He concurred I had the flu! Big deal – also said I would feel lousy for a few more weeks.

I'm so proud of you – you are doing so wonderfully well in school. My baby – well now you know what the Yiddish words *kvell* & *naches* mean.

I'm sure Ryan will strike it very big & rich real soon. So you'll buy a big house with a wing for me and I'll park there a few times a year and drive you all crazy.

The children sound good and happy. So do you. You know a lot can be heard in a voice.

Keep well – hope to see you all soon.

Now I'm going to pay my bills (UGH!)

Love to all –

Kisses to K & B

Mom

She could tell by my voice that I was happy. I sure had her fooled. And even though I was graduating college she was still confident my husband would get rich real soon? Hmmm.

Although I was glad Mom was excited about my graduation, I told her she needed to see a doctor right away, regardless of what her *friend* Ralph said. "This "flu" thing has gone on far too long."

"No," she told me. "I've waited this long, now I'll wait until after your graduation. I don't want to ruin your day." Looking back, I wonder if she had expected her prognosis would not be good.

I was proud of myself for doing so well in school, graduating with honors. It took me a while to get dressed. I stared in the mirror, adjusting the square mortarboard on my head, finally giving up trying to make it look good. Besides, my green gown, anything but flattering, would not be noticed amongst the hundreds, if not thousands, of graduates that would be attending the ceremony. Instead, I focused on the one item that would set me apart from the others. After I slipped my large medallion, indicating I'd achieved magna cum laude status, over my head, I stopped my primping as Mom handed me a store-bought graduation card. I opened it immediately, noticing a handwritten note inside.

> Dearest Joanie,
> I'm so proud of you! I knew you would make it and make it big. Just keep your sights high and you'll achieve anything you want because you have guts.
> I love you now, loved you then and I'll always love you because you're my baby – you'll always be my baby.
> June 15, 1986

As my jaw clenched, tightening up more than ever before, I could barely hold back my tears. Where are these words coming from? And why now? What about all the times she made me feel worthless? I always thought she hated me. That's the past. I need to let go of the past. I fixed my makeup, adjusted my cap and gown again, and hugged Mom so hard, I never wanted to let go. I couldn't tell her this whole graduation was for her benefit. Pretending we were a happy family was for her. Watching Ryan straighten his tie for the ceremony, I wondered if he even remembered my threat about getting a divorce after my graduation. He's got to realize I know he's still drinking.

I hadn't understood how sick Mom really was until I saw the pain in her face as she tried to sit through the ceremony. Having to stand most of the time, she was happy I was able to get special permission for her to be in the glass-enclosed room in the back of the Masonic Temple. Being in the room set aside for the president of the university and visiting dignitaries made her feel special. Watching her eyes well with tears of pride, rather than worry, made all my secrets worth it. I'm her little girl. I did well.

Mom made good on her promise to see her doctor right after my graduation. Definitely not the flu, she was scheduled for immediate exploratory surgery. After hours in the waiting room, the surgeon called my Aunt and me into his office to give us the news. It would be up to us to relay the information to her.

With no emotion in his voice, the doctor gave his entire speech without pause. Questions would be addressed later. "We found a melon-sized tumor attached to your mother's spine. It is inoperable. We can try to shrink it with radiation and chemotherapy. The prognosis? It's hard to say. We rarely see a tumor this size. And where it's situated, it's very painful. We will give her painkillers. We expect her to live anywhere between two weeks and two years."

Just like the diets that say you can lose "up to" ten pounds a week, I went with the "up to" theory. "What did the doctor tell you?" Mom asked the moment she awoke from the anesthesia.

I was honest. I held her hand, looked her in the eyes and said, "The doctor said you have up to two years to live."

I felt horrible that I had to go back home to Ohio. I wanted to be there for her. But in truth, there wasn't that much I could do. Right now she needed to live as normal a life as possible. That meant, without me there.

Now that I'd become closer to Mom, part of me wanted to confide in her. To tell her what I'd gone through. To have my mommy comfort me. Tell me she loves me. Tell me everything will work out fine. Remembering all those years ago, when she warned me not to marry Ryan, I wanted to tell her she was wrong. We didn't have problems because of our different religions, or because he grew up in a rural town and I grew up "outside of" New York. I wanted her to understand that once a person is educated, the playing field is leveled. He had an engineering degree. As a well-paid businessman, he should be accepted by all, including my mink-wearing mother.

In truth, she did accept her son-in-law. Not knowing anything about his addiction, she thought of him as a wonderful, hardworking, man. When we'd visit, and Ryan would pass out on the couch, my mother would order me to "leave the poor boy alone", not realizing he wasn't sleeping, he was drugged. I wanted Mom to know I couldn't stay in this marriage anymore because he was an addict and I wasn't. He drank and I didn't. I wanted a family life, he wanted to party. We wanted different things in life. I begged him to quit using, stop drinking. For our family. For himself. When I finally realized that wasn't going to happen, I had to let go.

"You have the right to do anything you want," I told my husband, right before my graduation, "but I don't have to accept your choices."

After Mom's diagnosis, however, everything changed. I needed to take care of her. I couldn't burden her with my problems. Ryan got an extension on my threat. He needed to clean up his act by the time my mom succumbed to the cancer, or I would file for a divorce.

Knowing I had responsibilities to my mom and my children, within a few weeks after graduation, I secured a part time job that allowed me the flexibility to be home by four in the afternoon, as well as travel back and forth to New Jersey to help Mom.

Sitting in the radiologist's office, hopeful one of Mom's many treatments would help, we actually started to lighten up and laugh. I think they call it gallows humor. It helps. "Why do they always describe tumors as fruit?" I asked, joking. Maybe serious. "The doctor told me the tumor was the size of a melon. Why wasn't he more specific? I pictured a cantaloupe. What if he meant a watermelon?"

"I would prefer a grapefruit," Mom said.

"Maybe after the radiation, it will shrink to a grapefruit." I added, with a smile.

"Actually," Mom said, raising her hand in a snobby way, "I would prefer a grape, thank you." We both laughed.

I think we both would have settled for an apple.

After the appointment, I took Mom out for ice cream as she had taken me out so many times after my dance and piano lessons. Besides shopping, it's what we did best.

Eventually, I needed to go back home. I needed to be with my young children, whom I left in the hands of God, not trusting Ryan at all. Between the radiation and the chemo, Mom seemed to be feeling better. At least she could sit for short periods of time without suffering. The Percocet helped a lot.

I continued traveling back and forth to New Jersey every few weeks. Trying to recreate the best moments of my childhood, I treated Mom to the Broadway musical *42nd Street*, we dined at her favorite restaurants and exercised my credit cards at Lord & Taylor and Bloomies in between the mandatory chemo and radiation treatments. And we talked like never before. We touched on politics, movies, TV, the kids, everything but my marriage. She never asked. I never complained.

The chemo had a wonderful side effect. Without trying, she was losing weight. We'd shop for fashionable warm up suits and found the perfect gold purse to carry her portable chemo pump. With no nausea, no hair loss, she was thrilled at the compliments she received as she grew thinner. "You never looked better," was her favorite, responding, "Had I known cancer was the perfect diet, I would have gotten it earlier."

As her only child, I felt obligated to be with Mom as much as possible. And I know she appreciated our time together. I'm not sure if the cancer had mellowed her. It didn't matter. We got along wonderfully. With fighting a distant memory, we actually had fun.

Mom took the whole ordeal in stride. I saw a new side of her as she joked with her doctors and kibitzed with other patients. "At my age I didn't think anyone would be interested in seeing my butt", Mom said to the Sharpie wielding nurse as she marked the target spot for the radiologist. "The next thing you know they'll be asking me to pose for Playboy."

I think I got my sense of humor from Mom. The more nervous I am, the funnier I get. "Laugh at your problems", my favorite mug reads. "Everyone else is."

We laughed. Her chemo and radiation brought us closer than ever.

She fought against starting morphine. Wanting to keep her mind sharp as long as possible, she resisted the drug, until she could no longer stand the pain. I don't know how long I'd been sitting in her hospital room, my legs wearing a groove in the faded vinyl, watching, anxiously waiting for Mom's face to relax, hoping for a sign that the pain killer was working. It's true what they say. Sometimes it is harder to watch someone else suffer. I wished I could take away some of her pain, but I couldn't. At least she was getting some rest now. With her asleep, I stayed by her bedside, thinking.

Looking back on my life, I think Mom really didn't like children. While my dad's face lit up like the Christmas tree at Rockefeller Center, my mom never seemed all that excited to have Brandon and Katie, or any kids, for that matter, in her house. She epitomized the expression; children should be seen and not heard. Come in, give Grandma a hug, eat your dinner, and then go to your room, or go watch TV.

It was Dad who got down on the floor and played cards and games, entertaining the little ones for hours. Mom stayed in the kitchen, cooking her chicken soup, preparing the dinner for the party that she would undoubtedly throw for us. I didn't complain. I looked forward to seeing those same characters, Rudy, Estelle, who attended all of her soirées since I was a child. Only there were fewer guests as the years passed. Widows and widowers, retelling the same stores I'd heard many times.

As a child, I had resented Mom's orders to clean up the kitchen as I cooked. When I started cooking for myself, with no one monitoring my every move, I made messes in the kitchen. OK, I trashed the kitchen. Leaving bowls, caked with dried up batter, sitting in the sink for hours, days, I felt liberated. Ha-ha! I thought. *No one's going to tell me what to do anymore.* The higher the dishes piled up, the more liberated I felt. *I'll clean the damn dishes when I feel like it!* That'll show her. I enjoyed not being told what to do. Unfortunately, my plan backfired. Each time I went to cook again, I couldn't find any dishes. The bowls, the glasses, the pots and pans, sat encrusted in the sink. Unusable. I couldn't move forward, I couldn't prepare a meal or set the table, until I took care of my mess from the last meal, or the previous day. Soon I learned that Mom was right. It is better to clean up as I go along. I do that now. I want to tell Mom that.

For two years I prayed to God, please, let the chemo work. We had grown so close since Dad passed away; I couldn't bear the thought of being without Mom, especially for the holidays. Selfishly thinking I'll never again taste her chicken soup, I wondered how I would ever enjoy a Passover, without her famous matzo balls, or her chopped liver. Or the fun we had gathered around the table, recalling, year after year the time someone accidentally switched the grape juice and the Manischewitz, and the kids got drunk. That was so much more memorable than the traditional story other families told of the Exodus, in which the ancient Israelites were freed from slavery in Egypt.

By the time she needed a morphine drip, I knew the end was near. I prayed for God to take away her pain.

Mom put much effort into apologizing to me during those weeks I sat at her bedside trying to comfort her after we realized the end to her two year battle with cancer was near. "I know I was a bitch to you," came as a surprise to me. I smiled, figuring it was probably the morphine talking, allowing her the freedom to let go of her pride for once in her life. "You were a lovable bitch", I responded, with a wink and a smile, while my heart was breaking inside. Why couldn't she have apologized years ago? Why do they always wait until their deathbed? It's like the parents who know their children are struggling financially, but refuse to loan them money when they need it, saving it, instead, for "the inheritance." By the time the will is read, the family is bitter and torn apart.

We both laughed. For the first time in years, maybe ever, we talked about the past. We both opened up. In this dreary hospital room, with its green walls, threadbare divider curtains,

IV drip, heartbeat monitor, this same hospital where Brandon was born, where Dad had died, for the first time in my memory, Sylvia, my mom, wasn't judgmental. Apologizing for how she treated me as a child, I wondered why she waited until she was dying. No one knew the pain I felt growing up. I kept quiet, not wanting to go into details about how much she had hurt me. Not now. She was dying. I let her talk.

A week before she died she told me about a "lock box" that was hidden in the back of the top shelf in her bedroom closet. "There are important papers in there." She said. Then she gave me the secret code. "Your daddy's birthday".

This was the first time I felt nervous being alone in Mom's house, my childhood home. Before this trip my only concerns involved the safety of my children and the quality of Mom's life. Leaving Brandon and Katie with their alcoholic father, I was placing my trust in God to watch over the three of them while I visited my dying mother. And now, I prayed that Mom's pain would end soon. As I prepared myself to open "the box, the secret hidden box" I felt my heart pounding in my throat.

Balancing on a chair pulled up to the bedroom closet, reaching past the stacks of hat boxes, the silk scarves and leather gloves, my hand touched the metal of a small box, like a buried treasure. I pulled the box down from the closet, placed it on her quilted bedspread and stared at it as I got comfortable in my usual position, legs tucked beneath me. Memories started flooding into my head like the waters crushing back together after Charlton Heston parted the Red Sea. Like it was yesterday, I pictured my Koko after giving birth, surrounded by her litter of eight poodles, resting on the blood stained blanket right there, in front of this same mirrored closet door.

I looked at the box. After taking a deep breath I rotated the first cylinder to "6". The second was already in the correct position. After easing the third cylinder into place I could feel the lid release and slowly open. Although I had no idea what was in this treasure chest, I knew it contained something important. I rifled through lots of papers. Mostly insurance docs. Itemized lists assigning values to her jewelry, furs, monogrammed silverware and the Herend China my dad shipped over from Hungary during the war. "My inheritance".

I smiled, thinking how although my parents weren't wealthy by any means, they liked their trinkets. As I worked my way through the documents I came to a sudden halt. My heart stopped. "Adoption Papers" – baby girl Stamberg. Oh my God. My birth name. I rested the folded pages on the bedspread, staring at them as if they were a prized possession awaiting valuation on the Antiques Roadshow.

My eyes burned as hot tears flowed down my cheeks into my mouth. I could hardly make out the words as my eyes filled, fogging over my contacts. After removing my lenses, I was able to read the hand typed court document drafted over thirty-four years ago. While I studied the pages, one memory came to mind.

The last time I asked Mom about my birth she yelled, "Don't ever ask me that again." Then she kicked a hole in our kitchen wall. Was she telling me where the box was now so I'd find the adoption papers and open a dialog? Was she ready to talk? She had apologized for being so mean to me all my life. She realized she had been unfair. But was she ready to talk? Is this why she told me about the box?

I returned to the hospital the next morning expecting her to address the box. Joanie, did you find the box, do you have any questions? I'm ready now to answer anything. No. She never mentioned the lock box and I didn't have the heart, or guts, to bring it up at this time. She was dying. I wasn't going to do or say anything that would upset her now. She had to be the one to broach the subject.

I don't know why, but no matter how many disappointments Sylvia had in her life, she could never bring herself to talk to me about her greatest disappointment of all – that she could not give birth. I said nothing.

That was Sylvia in a nutshell. She never let anyone inside. At least she never let me in. She hated that I was so different than her. Finding my adoption papers, I wondered again if Mom knew more than she was telling me. Did Sylvia know who my birthmother was? *Was I like my birthmother? Is that what she hated about me?* I'll never know. I learned a lot from her cruelty toward me, raising my children with positive reinforcement, not negative. I know they never doubted my love for them. The greatest compliment Mom ever gave me was "I know you're raising Brandon and Katie the opposite of how I raised you. I'm very proud of you".

Five years after my dad succumbed to heart disease and two years after she was diagnosed with cancer, I knew Mom would pass away soon. Perhaps her secrets were a sign of the times. People didn't "share" in those days like they do now. In an era in which one didn't utter the word "cancer", Mom would carry her secrets to the grave. In burying the woman who raised me, I would have to accept as fact I would be putting to rest any hope of finding the woman who gave me life.

CHAPTER EIGHT

I had read once that when a person is dying the most important thing we can do for them is to let them talk. Normally quiet around Mom, her last few weeks, I chatted more than ever, trying to keep her spirits up. Mom even remarked how she'd never heard me say so much in my life. I was on a roll. We gossiped about movie stars, bantered about politics. I told her the kids were getting A's. I never mentioned Ryan at all. I especially didn't want her to know that I suspected he had used cocaine, and might have tried the new drug "crack" that I'd read about. She didn't need to know that.

I also let her talk. She never brought up the lock box again. However, she did talk about her funeral, letting me know she wanted to be buried the same way my father was buried. She wanted to have an Orthodox Jewish service with a simple pine coffin.

After they could do no more for her at the hospital, they sent Mom home, to die. When she knew her end was near, with her home health aide at her side, she hosted her final party. Our little family was summoned to her bedside, for one last visit. Dressed in a new peignoir set and propped up with at least a dozen throw pillows as if she were a queen on her throne, Mom proceeded to distribute a few of her prized possessions, including my dad's sword collection from the war.

The call came early the next morning after I returned home from my final visit. Practically throwing the kids in the car, I first had to find Ryan, already at the golf course, and drive the seven hour trip back to the hospital. Upon our arrival, at the front desk, the receptionist had us take a seat while the nurse checked on Mom to see if she was ready for our visit. Waiting in the lobby, we were anxious to get up to her room, before it was too late.

A moment later, the nurse returned, telling us Mom had just passed away a minute before. She knew we were here. I have no doubt she waited until she knew we had arrived at the hospital safely, before she let go.

As her only child, it was my sole responsibility for the plans from that moment on. Ignoring my uncle's suggestion to have a "convenient" funeral in Lake Hiawatha, I insisted on giving Mom the funeral she wanted. An orthodox Jewish service like my dad's.

Looking through her files, I found all the information I needed for the service and the obituary. Since my mom rarely attended synagogue anymore, the Rabbi came to our house to learn as much as he could to prepare his eulogy.

Brandon and Katie stayed in the guest room while Ryan and I, along with my Aunt and Uncle, gathered in the faux wood-grain paneled TV room, the room that had once been my bedroom, my hideout. My sanctuary. I turned my back away from the full-length mirror, still on the door, where I spent so much time crouched, silently listening to Mom's endless rants in the kitchen. I'm sure she didn't really think I was a bad person. Or that no one would ever like me. Maybe she was menopausal and we didn't realize it.

As the Rabbi asked questions about Mom, everyone recalled a funny story. We talked about our famous Seder, when the kids got drunk on Manischewitz while the adults complained their "wine" had no kick. We talked about the party girl she was and her famous matzo balls. How she rescued a kitten from chocking on my bracelet, the one we named Vaseline in honor of Mom's brilliant idea for removing the jewelry. Everyone agreed Mom's Mandelbrot and chopped liver were to die for. No one mentioned anything bad. Only the good.

During the funeral, sitting in the front row, flanked by my husband and children, all dressed up in their best clothes, we listened as Rabbi Savitz related those same stories to a crowded room. Her party guests. Cousins I hadn't seen in years. Surviving members of my dad's family. Even neighbors I hadn't met came to say goodbye to Sylvia. Every one of them told me how my mom always talked about me. How proud she was of me. Why didn't she ever tell me that? Why did she let me spend so much of my life thinking she hated me?

My divorce was final in November 1988, two months after Mom's funeral. I think giving Ryan sixteen years of my life was enough time to get fixed. To quit the drinking. The drugs. He didn't change. Probably once I threatened I'd divorce him after my mother died, he gave up.

Now was the time for me to change my life. Armed with a degree, I needed to move on, to plan for a full-time job once I was done dealing with Mom's house. My life had been so crazy the past few years taking care of Mom that I'd totally let myself go. Living on potato chips and ice cream, I desperately needed to lose weight. I'd done it before. When the children were little I joined Weight Watchers and reached my goal weight. Now, at my highest weight ever, I needed to join again. I needed to take care of myself. I could do it. Just one more Sara Lee cheesecake and I'm ready to go.

Finally, after New Year's, I stuffed myself into the one pair of jeans I could squeeze on, topped it with a new pink turtleneck, and sat through the longest hour of my life. But I did it. I stuck with the program, determined to reach my goal.

***

When I heard the phone ringing in the middle of the night, I never expected it to be my ex-husband. I pulled my pillow over my head, tucked the handset under my ear and whispered "Hello?"

Silence. Then I heard breathing. Knowing someone was there I tried again. "Hello? Who is this?" I whispered louder.

"Joanie?"

I hadn't heard that voice in months. It took me so long to finally be able to fall asleep at night without worrying if he was dead or alive.

"Yes." I answered. Although my heart was racing, I dared not ask questions.

"It's bad, I'm bad. I mean…Please, come and get me."

Had my worst nightmare occurred? Is this the moment I'd been dreading all these years? My mind spun, wondering if I still had the funeral plans I was always working on. I vaguely recall him saying something about wanting his ashes scattered on a golf course.

I couldn't believe this is happening again. I thought our divorce meant an end to my involvement in his drama. No more bailing him out of jail at all hours, no more retrieving him from bars. Isn't that the main benefit of a divorce? I can move on with my life without being sucked in again? Propping myself up on my elbow, I reached for the light switch and grabbed a pen and pad off my night table. Taking a deep breath I asked, "Where are you?"

The address he gave me was somewhere near the high school. Going into autopilot mode as I'd done so many times before, I tugged on a pair of sweats and threw a hoodie over my nightgown. I hated leaving Brandon and Katie without telling them where I was going. But I couldn't. Why should they have to worry too? Besides, I might be back before they even wake up. I had no idea how long this would take. They might need to make their own breakfast before school. I left a brief note on the kitchen table. "Be back soon. Make PB&J for your lunch. Love you!" I didn't know how I'd explain this later.

An eerie calm took over my body as I recalled the sense of peace I felt the minute I accepted him for what he was, an addict. Not a bad person, not a criminal, he was a human being afflicted with an addiction. It took me so many years to understand I could not fix him. It was not my job to change him or cure him. At the same time I learned my limitations I also began to realize I didn't have to accept his behavior. I didn't have to spend the rest of my life living in fear under the same roof with him. I had choices. I could choose to lead my own life, without the addict. It was the simple act of giving up that set me free. My decision to divorce was not made lightly. But it was the first decision I made for me and my children. It was the first right choice I'd made in a long time.

Operating on pure adrenaline like the mother pulling her child from a burning car, I didn't stop to analyze the possibility of danger as I quietly eased my gold Nova out of the garage. It was 3:20 AM and I prayed I wouldn't draw attention to myself. The last thing I needed now was to test out our neighborhood watch association. As I continued down the barren streets in a dreamlike state, I felt like I was watching a movie of myself going through the motions. What's one more night heading to God-knows-where rescuing him from God-knows-what? He always survives.

As I pulled onto East 222nd Street, I didn't recognize the person hunched over on the curb. With no car, ratty clothes, greasy hair, he could have been any homeless person wielding a sign that says "will work for food". I pretended this isn't really happening. It's easier to think of myself acting out a scene from a movie. I imagined I was rescuing Nicolas Cage from his suicide bender in *Leaving Las Vegas*. That didn't work. I knew it wasn't true. This was not 'any' homeless person. It killed me to admit that this man on the brink of death is the father of my children, my husband of sixteen years. My ex. Our days of fighting meant we cared enough to work out our differences. What scared me now was how I felt nothing, empty.

He eased his body slowly into my passenger seat like he was afraid he would break. I could tell he was in pain but I avoided eye contact. I ignored the greasy hair, the foul smell. It's too late for lectures. Where's that handsome man I dressed up in Calvin Klein and Ralph Lauren? Did I really believe expensive clothing would improve his self-esteem? Turn him into a respectable business man? I didn't know this person. Maybe I never did. I wondered if he had finally hit bottom. Who knows? Every time I thought he couldn't sink any lower he proved me wrong.

The stench of cigarettes, alcohol, probably pot, became overwhelming. I noticed that the wrinkled papers he gripped were discharge papers from the hospital.

"I need you to take me to Laurelwood drug treatment center," he said, staring straight ahead. He couldn't make eye contact either. "The address is on the first page." He handed me the sheets.

"OK," I answered, with no judgment in my voice. I accepted that he needed one more binge. I hoped this is the last. I remained silent as I moved the gear shift into drive, checked my rear view mirror, and pulled out into the street. Another rehab. I was not going to get my hopes up that this time it would work. That this time he would get clean and sober.

During the short drive to Willoughby I recalled how I used to feel when I looked into his eyes. Those eyes that would make my heart melt while his smile unlocked the key to my soul. Those eyes that promised he was telling me the truth when his actions told a different story. Now all that remained are colorless discs, devoid of life. It's the drugs. They killed him. The drugs are what destroyed a man and left this lump sitting on the curb like trash the garbage men refused to pick up.

As I walked down the hospital's green hallways, I welcomed the smell of disinfectant that momentarily distracted my senses from the smoke and alcohol. I explained to deaf ears that we're divorced, he's not my responsibility. They made me sign anyway. I detected a barely audible "thank you" before the attendant took his elbow and lead him down the corridor. No one looked back. My job was done.

Safely back in my garage by six, I sneaked in the house

before the kids woke up. I tore up my note hoping they'd never find out what happened tonight. I prepared peanut butter and jelly sandwiches and took a nice hot bath before their alarms went off at six-thirty.

After Brandon and Katie had breakfast and caught the bus, I hopped back into my car and sprayed it down with Lysol. I was ready to start my real day. Back in the bathroom I dabbed some extra cover cream below my eyes and applied two coats of mascara before I pulled on my favorite royal blue dress, the one with the wide belt that accentuated my tiny waist.

Entering the meeting hall this time was different. Instead of stopping at the scale, or relaxing in my usual seat at the far left side of the second row, close to the rest rooms, I continue walking toward the back of the room. Opening the door I find a group of well-dressed attractive women chatting away at the rectangular table. I notice everyone is already settled in with coffee. I quickly grab a cup and head over to the table.

"Great, Joanie's here. If you'll take your seat we can get started." I grab a chair at the end of the table. Lucretia begins...

"I want to welcome everyone to our first day of training to be a Weight Watchers leader. Let's go around the room and everyone can introduce themselves and tell each other a little about ourselves."

The teacher, the mother, the party planner...finally it's my turn.

"Hi everyone. I'm Joanie." *Oh my God*, I think. What can I tell them? *I can't just blurt out, I just got in from rescuing my ex from a suicide mission and I have two children?* I decide to tell the truth. I continue.... "I have two wonderful children and since losing 40 pounds on the Weight Watchers program....I'm confident I can do anything. I'm so happy to be here! I can't wait to start my training."

When I get home I collapse. The first day at my new job will surely be memorable.

In seven short weeks my leaders training was complete and I was ready for my very own meeting. I was nervous. The room was packed. The official count, eighty-two. My heart was racing. After I weighed in the last member at the scale, my receptionist took over so I could go to the front of the room. It seemed like forever as I stood in the wings, watching the clock, waiting for the minute hand to jump to the twelve for my meeting to start at 7:00, on the dot. I jogged out to my "stage" like I was Jay Leno, about to give a monologue. Except, instead of Jay, they got treated to a Joan Rivers wannabe. I was on! I felt alive. For once, I was in my element. I was self-confident. I looked great. I shared my story of my love for food. My passion for ice cream. How it was disappearing, gallon by gallon, and it was all me. I couldn't blame anyone else, but myself. They nodded their heads. They related. I found something I was good at. Finally. I answered members' questions with expertise. I was good.

After the meeting, the new members came up to the front of the room, excited to learn about the program. They hung on every word I said. I asked each one to introduce himself or herself so I could get to know everyone. I stop at one member who is obviously not happy. Refusing to give me her name. I ask "Why?"

"You know me." She said. "I sat in the front row for the entire meeting waiting for you to acknowledge me."

Honestly, I'd never seen this woman before in my life. "I'm sorry." I told her. "Please tell me your name."

Very apologetic, she told me she thought I was someone else, swearing I looked identical to someone she knew. Did I have a twin? I wondered? Last week at 84 Lumber, someone said to me "You should know where (a certain tool) is. You're in here all the time." Maybe I really do have a twin. More than ever I was determined to pursue my adoption story. I was desperate to know the truth.

I don't know how to start. How do I find out more about my birth?

CHAPTER NINE

Every few months I drove back to New Jersey, to check up on Mom's house. To clean the cabinets, clear out the clutter. I had difficulty deciding what to do with the property. There was always a chance I might want to move back there. But that would mean taking twelve year old Brandon and eleven year old Katie far away from their father. I wasn't ready to make that decision. Most likely I would sell the house after the unveiling of Mom's grave.

I walked through the rooms like I was touring a museum, stopping outside each doorway as if it were roped off. I'd stare inside, not wanting to disturb anything. Mom's bed was covered with her favorite bedspread, the pillows lined up just as she liked them. In the living room, my piano rested quietly against the wall, underneath the Renoir. I smiled when I came to Mom's gold-flock wallpapered dining room, wondering what she was thinking when she picked that design. I chose to focus on the happy moments I spent with my mom.

Cleaning out Mom's basement, I was taken aback when I discovered, next to the upright freezer, a large soup spoon resting in a clean juice glass on the rusted metal utility table she used for stacking laundry. I opened the freezer section to see what she might have tasted with that spoon. I noticed a vintage harvest gold Tupperware container marked "liver". Hating liver, I never looked inside before. Expecting to find a freezer burnt cow organ, I was surprised to discover a half empty box of Breyers Coffee Ice Cream. Sylvia, we had more in common than either of us realized.

Divorced for several months now, I learned Ryan, upon embarking in another round of rehab, provided my name as his "next of kin". Although I remembered agreeing to attend the hospital's family night program, I didn't understand why Katie, Brandon, and I, had to sit amongst strangers, listening to addicts give their drug-a-logs. It was his turn. Ryan was standing before the group preparing to present his story. As he read from his yellow legal pad, I got the distinct feeling he was proud of his accomplishments. Proud that his list was longer than the other addicts. Valium, Quaaludes, pot, heroin, crack, 8-balls, cocaine...I lost count very quickly. I'd never heard of most of these drugs. Did he say Percocet? Wasn't that the medication my mother was taking for her cancer? Yes, he just told everyone he was stealing Mom's pain killers. It sounded more like he was reading from *The Physicians' Desk Reference*. Had he gotten a medical degree that I didn't know about?

My mind drifted. When did he do this? Why didn't I know? I thought alcohol was the problem. He told me he rarely drank anymore. I didn't believe him. Now, I'm wondering when he would even have had time to drink if he was taking all these drugs. Maybe I could have used some for my diet. He never offered to share. I kept sending him to doctors to find out what was wrong with him. Why was he so tired? I was worried all the time about his health. But he always made it to work. At least I thought he did. Even after he was diagnosed with Hepatitis B, and I had to take a series of painful vaccinations, he still said he went into work every day.

And those business trips. He's telling everyone in the room he wasn't taking the business trips. They were more like drug runs. I didn't know. I feel so stupid. Naïve. Why hadn't he lost his job? They obviously didn't know either. What was he telling his boss? Was he calling in sick? I'm so confused. I see him sitting down now. I don't know what to say. I can't look at him. Looking around the room I felt so out of place. In my Dockers, turtleneck top and cardigan sweater, I'm not fancy. But I'm so different than the others in their ripped jeans and steel-toed shoes, some wearing wife beaters, others in plaid flannel; many looked like they hadn't had a good meal in weeks let alone carry a Saks credit card like I do. How did this nice Jewish girl from Jersey wind up in a hospital group on the west side of Cleveland? I don't belong. I have to get out.

Why did I ever think he'd change? We were from different worlds. I look around the room again. I bet these people don't even know what Manischewitz is, or for that matter what a Jew is. They probably are all high on something themselves. I need to leave. I don't belong. I wonder if it is my imagination or are most of the group members missing teeth.

I wring my hands and take a deep breath as Hannah, the rehab counselor, gently touches my arm and guides the three of us over to sit on some folding chairs in the more private rear of the family meeting room. She wants to explain the situation to us. Looking like a baby in her pink scrubs, I guess Hannah can't be much older than twenty. What could she possibly know about addiction? She's just going by what they teach them in books. She doesn't have any idea what it feels like to live with an addict. She's probably still waking up in her frilly little pink bedroom in her parents' house. They are probably still paying her bills. Why should I listen to her? But what choice do we have? We'd certainly tried everything else.

"We don't usually tell our families this..." Hannah takes a deep breath, obviously uncomfortable. "But we feel it is important for you to know." *Who is this "we" she's talking about?* "We've never seen an addict in as bad a condition as your husband, (I want to remind her he's my ex-husband) both physically and mentally. In our opinion, we feel in all likelihood he is not going to make it. He is going to die."

I'm not exactly sure what she is telling me. Although living in separate households, we still share a business, children, and I continue to control the finances. The three of us are his only support, physical, mental and financial. He needs us to survive. He has no one else to turn to. So when the phone call came and I literally picked his carcass off the street and hauled him into another round of treatment, we were again sucked into his drama. I'd like to say being involved with him again is against my better judgment, but apparently I have no judgment at all.

"We're not married anymore. I don't know what I'm supposed to do," I tell Hannah. "I've done everything I could. He's not my problem anymore."

"We feel you should let him come back home. Let him come back home so he can die with his family around him."

This was too much for me to handle. How is it possible I didn't know about all those drugs? About his missing work? I'm such a fool. Now they want me to take him back into my home. It's not his home anymore. He chose drugs over us. We gave him so many chances, but each time he chose the drugs. We are finally starting to get used to living, or trying to live, on our own. Without controversy. Without drama. It feels good to come and go without worrying for a change. Now she's asking us, telling us, that we need to bring this addict back into our house. This is truly insane.

Every fiber of my being screamed "NO!! Don't do it." But, again, against all my instincts, I acquiesced. I did as I was told. I allowed Ryan to move back into my home, to die. But he didn't die. Once again, in the honeymoon phase of treatment, he made his usual promises. "I won't….." "I'll never….." "I've changed….." "Trust me…." No longer believing anything he said, I was on constant high alert, always waiting for the other shoe to fall. Again, my heart raced each time I'd drive down the street toward my house. Before pulling into the driveway, I would worry. Will he be home? Will he be sober? What if his car isn't there? Where could he be? Is he dead yet?

Living with a drug addict is all consuming. Getting caught up in the sickness again, I was determined to fix him. To protect him. If we love him enough, he won't want to use drugs anymore. We'll prove he has something to live for. This was definitely insane. How many times could I do the same thing and expect different results? It became difficult leaving the house to go grocery shopping. "Take care of daddy while I'm gone," I'd instruct my young children. I hid his car keys. I locked away my money. But I was still nervous. I spent my days waiting for him to die or get "fixed", whichever came first. Soon, I became consumed with protecting my children.

Lying to my children would be a more accurate description. "Keep quiet. Daddy's sick. He needs his rest", I'd tell them when their dad had been in bed for days. By night, I became the liquor cabinet monitor. (I know. Why was there even a liquor cabinet in the house?) Worrying about his impending death consumed every moment of my days. No longer responsible for pouring alcohol down the drain, or flushing drugs down the toilet, my job, I was told, was to bring him home to die. If taking the drugs and alcohol was going to help him die, so be it. But he wasn't dying. Even though I was hiding the money, he seemed to be using again. He seemed to be getting worse. We were getting worse. I start kissing him "hello" to see if I detected alcohol on his breath, but he always seemed to smell like Halls Mentho-Lyptus. Was the menthol cough drop a cover for the alcohol? I began marking the level on the liquor bottles and the mouth wash. Eventually I reached the point where I no longer let the kids come home after school if I was not home. They were to go directly to a friend's house and wait until I picked them up.

This wasn't living. Waiting for someone to die, hoping, praying, that he didn't bring us down with him was devastating. I worried the kids would find Ryan's dead body on the floor, with a needle stuck in his arm. I worried the kids would find his drugs and try them. I spent every moment of every day obsessing, "what if". Every night, while Ryan slept on my couch, I lay in bed planning his funeral. This was not how I had envisioned life after divorce.

Again, we attended AA meetings. Once more, I felt out of

place. We argued about which meeting to go to. I wanted to go to the nice Jewish AA meetings where they served fresh, cream-filled Dunkin Donuts. He preferred the toothless AA meetings with coffee and stale cookies. I returned to my Al-Anon meetings. My Al-Anon friend's husband became Ryan's sponsor. I had a social life. We hung out with our Al-Anon and AA friends. Everything would be fine. As long as he stayed sober. He didn't. I went back to waiting for him to die, as the counselor instructed me.

In the meantime, I took care of myself, teaching Weight Watchers, staying on my diet, and attending four or five Al-Anon meetings per week. They were very helpful. The Al-Anon members didn't care about curing the addict. They didn't even want to hear about the addict. They didn't care that if he no longer used drugs, drank, we'd have money, and we wouldn't have to worry about paying his outrageous insurance premiums. That we'd be like a normal family, or at least a normal divorced family. They ignored my insisting on fixing the addict to make us better. They just wanted to hear about me! Again, they told me, "Keep coming back."

Eventually I got it through my head that Ryan was not the problem. It was me. I needed to fix me!

That Serenity Prayer, "God, grant me the serenity to accept the things I cannot change; the courage to change the things I can; and the wisdom to know the difference", was saying I needed to have enough wisdom to learn I can't change others. I can only change myself.

I did as they said. I kept coming back. And back. I embraced "Let go let God." "One day at a time." "Progress not perfection." These words started to have meaning. My constant checking up on him was not going to stop him from taking drugs. Why should I stop living my life just because he was messed up? Didn't I have a right to be happy? Where was it written that my happiness depended upon him? Isn't self-esteem about self? It was not my job to fix him. It was his job. My job was to fix me. To be strong. To be a good mother.

No longer alone, I found others who listened. Who'd been

there. Who'd survived. Who made a life for themselves. Some of these men and women were still with their addict. Others had divorced. Some found a new addict. Others broke the cycle. I embraced my new social life. My dysfunctional social life.

Hanging out at Bob Evans for our nightly, after meeting, meeting, we tried to put the fun in dysfunctional. Occasionally we even managed to talk about things other than the addict. I had no idea there were any other topics. But there were. Things were actually happening in the world. There were TV programs and movies that had themes other than curing your addict. I laughed. I began to find humor in my pain. "Addict comes home from bar. Wife asks, "How did you get the black eye?" Addict answers, "The bar popped up and hit me in the face." When Ryan told me that story I rolled my eyes and told him he was sick. When I "shared" my story at Bob Evans over our bottomless pots of coffee, we were all holding our stomachs laughing. I actually laughed myself. It felt good.

I shopped. It had been so long since I'd bought anything for myself. Always making sure there was enough money for the DUI attorneys, the high risk auto insurance, his car payments for the new car he purchase after totaling the last one, I hadn't thought about buying clothes for myself in ages. I went to town with some killer jeans and tight sweaters. Having lost weight since the divorce, I looked hot. I kind of liked when that Barry Manilow look-a-like started hitting on me at our social hours. I had almost forgotten I was divorced. I was a free agent. Wasn't I? Why not go for it? Even if just to make Ryan jealous. Maybe then he'd see what he would be missing if he didn't get his act together.

I learned there actually is life after addiction. And that life would be with or without the addict. It was my choice. The most important lesson I learned was: I have the right to change my mind. Yes, I brought him home to die. But I could change my mind. And change my mind I did. Eventually.

Mom had been gone a year. I'd decided I would sell her house and remain in the Cleveland area since the cost of living was lower. And Brandon and Katie had friends in the neighborhood. Besides, I still hoped Ryan would recover.

Even though he was living with me at the time, I didn't bring Ryan back home for the unveiling of Mom's headstone. I didn't want to ruin the last party I'd ever throw in the home where I'd grown up.

It was time to revisit the cemetery. Looking at the joint headstone, now listing Mom's name alongside my dad's name, I felt a pang of guilt, wiping a tear from my eye, selfishly thinking I'd never again taste her chicken soup. Wondering, if it was such good medicine, why couldn't it cure her cancer?

The crowd was smaller this time. Just my Aunt, Uncle, cousins and a few friends. We went back to Mom's house after Rabbi Savitz's graveside service. Platters of turkey and lox, and bagels and cream cheese, adorned the dining room table. It almost felt like old times. Just one person was missing. But she was still the star of the day.

I don't know how we got on the topic of my adoption. Maybe I mentioned the lock box. Finding my adoption papers. I just remember staring at my plate, not touching a bite of food, and reminiscing how I always knew I was adopted and that Mom told me my birth mother had died in childbirth.

"No she didn't," my aunt interrupted. "Your birth mother handed you to your father."

She must be wrong, I thought, but this wasn't the time to start an argument. I got quiet, remembering spending quite a bit of time at my Aunt Naomi's house growing up because that's where my Grandma lived. I recalled how my aunt would point out that I was short and chubby, like her. I never let her know how it hurt me whenever she'd make it clear to anyone seeing us that the little blonde girl was her daughter, telling them I was "Sylvia's kid".

Now, after a service for my mom, I'm wondering why my aunt would say such a thing to me about my birth. She must have known that my mom told me, no, insisted, that my birth mother died in childbirth. I grew up believing I killed my birth mother. I asked her one question. "Do you know anything else?"

"She was an older woman. That's all I know," my aunt added, as matter-of-factly as if she were telling me my mom preferred Nova Scotia lox over belly lox. She reached for her cigarette from Mom's Cinzano ashtray, inhaled deeply and turned to talk to someone else. It was obvious she either didn't realize or didn't care that this information changed everything I had believed my entire life.

I couldn't deal with this now. There were guests to attend to. Food to serve.

As soon as everyone left, I went back to cleaning the house, getting it ready to sell, trying to take my mind off my ex-husband, at home, doing God-knows-what. On top of that, I'm back to obsessing about my birth. If my birth mother didn't die, I need to find out what really happened. Why did Mom lie to me all these years? And why would my birth mother hand me to my father? Why wouldn't she hand me to my mother? The baby always goes to the mother. There must be some kind of mistake. My Aunt was wrong.

Following the unveiling, my trip back to Ohio was long and exhausting. We started our drive in the evening, hoping to stop at a hotel when I got tired. When we learned that all the hotels in Eastern Pennsylvania were booked due to a Penn State football game, Brandon and Katie fell asleep in the back seat of the car as I continued to drive through the night.

I could barely keep my eyes open let alone enjoy the brilliant pinks and blues that painted the sky as I neared my neighborhood. Pulling into the driveway at 5:30 AM, reality snapped me awake as if I was startled from a dream. My hands began trembling and my heart pounded in my throat at the sight of my garage door, literally hanging by one hinge, looking like it would fall to the ground at any moment. My beautiful house looked as if it belonged on a street of boarded up crack houses rather than a neighborhood of manicured lawns, white picket fences and freshly planted flower gardens. Something was terribly wrong. Much worse than usual. Thank God the kids were still asleep and didn't see anything. After futilely punching the remote door button, I placed the car in park, leaving the motor running. I quietly eased my cramped legs out of the car and followed a trail of blood to the garage. Operating purely on adrenalin, I gathered all my strength, forced the double door back into place until it was fully opened, returned to my Nova and coasted the vehicle into my parking space. I didn't even look to see the damage to Ryan's car as I gently awakened the kids and sent them to bed.

I had no idea what was awaiting me as I stepped through the doorway. I couldn't tell from the outside if what I saw was the scene of an accident or a crime. Since there was no yellow tape blocking off the drive, I assumed it was the scene of an accident. At this point I had no sympathy left for Ryan. Whatever happened, I assumed it was his fault.

Very quietly, so I wouldn't disturb Brandon and Katie, I nudged my snoring ex off my living room couch. "We need to talk, now." I guess he realized I was serious as he dragged his ass into the sunroom without complaining. Noticing a surgical bandage on his forehead and blood stains on his tee shirt, I tried to control my temper whispering, "What the fuck happened this time?"

"I drove into the garage door. Don't worry. The neighbors took me to the hospital." Worry was the last thing on my mind.

"And why did you drive into the garage door?" I asked with no hint of concern in my voice. I was beyond my limit. I have no idea if he even answered the question at this point. This game was over.

Letting someone stay in my house because they are terminally ill is one thing. But this was his last straw. It took me a long time but I finally got it....I have the right to change my mind. If he is going to die, let him die somewhere else. Not on my watch. He was putting our lives in jeopardy. What if the kids had been in the garage when he drove through the door? I've played the good guy long enough. Time to put an end to this. He needs to leave. Now!

Sitting on the couch in the sunroom, gathering all the

strength I had to carry on a conversation, I looked him straight in his blood shot eyes and enunciated very clearly, "You have to go. Now. You can't live here anymore." I didn't want to be misunderstood.

"I understand. You've given me enough chances." Ryan said with resignation in his voice. "I will look for another place to live this week."

"No. You don't understand. You will leave now."

"I don't have a place to go. I'll find a place tomorrow."

He really loved golf. His new set of Walter Hagens was his pride and joy. Perhaps his only pride and joy. Until now he hadn't noticed I was holding the three-wood that might have helped him achieve his most recent hole-in-one. I wouldn't hit him with the clubs. He knew I'm smarter than that. *Don't leave marks.* Isn't that what they always say? *Don't leave evidence.* Even at my wit's end, I still had the sense not to do anything that would jeopardize my future. He was not worth going to jail for. I wasn't going to risk losing my children because of him.

"You're leaving now," I said as I rolled the three-wood between the palms of my hands, feeling the cool lightness of the shaft.

"What are you doing? Give me that club." His eyes darted back and forth looking anxious.

"You are leaving now." It was easier to snap that club in half than I thought it would be. I tossed the two pieces to the side of the room. Like the next ball queuing up in a pinball machine, it seemed like another club just appeared in my hand, ready and waiting in the event he gave me another argument.

"Give me those clubs! I promise I'll look for another place to stay first thing in the morning. I need more sleep now."

Didn't he know his promises meant nothing to me anymore? How many times could I hear "I won't drink"? "I won't use"? I was sick and tired of being sick and tired. I could go through the entire bag of clubs if necessary. Hell, I'd spent so much time searching these pockets for drugs; why not clear out a few clubs while I'm at it? This was feeling good. I was getting my second wind. Maybe I'd find more evidence, just in case he wasn't getting my point.

Breaking the next club over my knee was a "snap". "It gets easier the more I break. I'm not stopping until you leave," I told him.

"Just give me the clubs. I promise I'll leave." As he started to reach for the clubs I began to break another with more force, and pleasure.

"Now." I said calmly, smiling with pleasure as I broke the third club.

He couldn't take it anymore. Grabbing the bag, he ran with it out to what was left of his car.

"You've got five minutes to get all your clothes out of here or I'm calling the police."

I think he finally realized I was serious. Since he had never really unpacked his 30-gallon Glad bag luggage from his last move, the packing was easy.

I had no more tears left at this point. I had already reached my personal bottom. I was cried out when I finally faced the reality that the man I fell in love with at eighteen, the man I thought I knew, had died years ago. The eyes that stared back at me were blank discs. I saw nothing but an empty shell of the man I once promised to spend the rest of my life with. I too was an empty shell. At that point, all life was drained out of me.

They say a marriage is over when the fighting ends. It's true. When there's nothing left to fight about or fight for, all hope is gone. Acceptance sets in.

Gazing out my picture window from my living room couch, that same window I'd looked through with apprehension so many years ago as Brandon and Katie boarded their first bus for kindergarten, and the one I often stared out of for hours during the wee hours of the morning waiting for the husband who promised he'd be home for dinner, I felt relief for the first time in years. I had no more tears left to shed as I sat in silence, watching his dented silver Honda Civic back out of the driveway for the last time. When it finally disappeared from view, I curled up in my bed and enjoyed the best sleep ever. First order of business after I awake, change the locks.

CHAPTER TEN

Letting Ryan move back home after rehab, even though we were divorced, was the right thing to do. All of my what-ifs were answered. I no longer had to wonder whether I had given him enough opportunities to quit drinking. To stop using drugs. After giving him this last chance, I was confident I did my best. I tried everything. Beyond everything. No one would ever fault me. Finally able to let go, I moved on.

Rather than feeling betrayed, I felt empowered. No longer whining about how much my husband hurt me, I embraced my Al-Anon tools to understand that Ryan did the best he could. As an addict, he was not strong enough to stop his insanity. However, I was. I decided I would not, under any circumstances, make the same mistake again. When I was ready to find love, I would not choose an addict. Well, maybe a garden variety alcoholic would be ok, but no drugs. I have my limits.

First things first, as I learned in Al-Anon, I needed to take care of myself and my children. Since Mom's house sold quickly and a lot of her furniture was now in my home, it would be quite a while before I had to worry about money. After paying off my mortgage, I took Brandon and Katie on a shopping spree. We stocked up on clothes, toys and I splurged on a state-of-the-art treadmill for me. I felt no guilt whatsoever! Still working at Weight Watchers, I was determined to keep in shape. Time for dating!

It didn't take long for me to fall in love again. When I first met Peter, I was swept away by his larger-than-life personality. He ate, shopped and traveled with gusto, apparently enjoying life to its fullest. No longer saddled with an alcoholic, I could go out, relax, and have fun. No more smelling someone's breath for alcohol. No more counting drinks. No more worrying the server would add vodka to our beverages by "accident". When Peter asked if I'd ever had sushi, I jumped at the chance for a new experience.

It was our second date, and my first Japanese meal that did not involve death-defying, knife-wielding chefs slicing and dicing my shrimp dangerously close to some of my favorite vital organs. After removing our shoes, we awkwardly tucked our legs beneath the traditional low-to-the-ground table in the rear of the strip-mall restaurant. After settling into the sunken booth, I prepared myself for a new experience. Confused by the unfamiliar terms on the menu, I shied away from the raw fish, accepting my date's suggestion to order a Philadelphia Roll, an Asian version of lox and cream cheese, hold the bagel. That sounded safe. Peter "started" by selecting a California Roll. Expecting an awkward pause after our orders were placed, I was impressed by Peter's instructions on the art of using chopsticks. "Don't worry," he said, smiling at my awkward attempts to follow his directions on grasping the two sticks. "You'll be an expert in no time." We laughed as I made a face taking my first sip of warm Sake. By my third sip I began to think, *I could get used to this*.

The one Philadelphia Roll was a perfect portion for me. I enjoyed the creamy texture and surprised myself by how fast I caught on to using chopsticks. As I was halfway through my meal and Peter had cleaned his plate, I expected he would wait for me to finish my portion and summon the check so we could leave. He didn't. His first order was, as they say, a good start. Watching the kimono-clad waitresses parade endless wooden platters of colorful California Rolls, Dragon Rolls and Rainbow Rolls to our table as if they were serving a feast to King Henry VIII, I convinced myself this excessive food consumption might not be as bad as it looked. Surely this man doesn't eat this much all the time. Maybe he was nervous, like I was. Maybe he was trying to impress me with his knowledge of Japanese food, or his expertise with the chopsticks. I shouldn't let this bother me. It's just one date. Besides, as long as he wasn't overdoing alcohol or using drugs, I could deal with it. Especially, being a Weight Watchers leader, a professional in dealing with food addictions, and a food addict myself, I shouldn't fault others for occasionally overindulging. Besides, he didn't look too overweight. Ten or twenty pounds on a man are nothing. As I continued to savor my one Philadelphia Roll, politely refusing additional servings, I sat back and watched the show, not saying anything. I, more than anyone, knew that pointing out someone's flaws rarely helps.

I accepted Peter's marriage proposal for the same reason I married Ryan. He said he loved me. More than that, he treated me special. He proudly introduced me to his friends. I liked his friends. They liked me. For the first time in years I had a social life that didn't involve meetings. Or steps. Or prayers. Everything seemed good. No, perfect. What could go wrong? I not only hopped on board for the ride of my life, I took Brandon and Katie along with me. New York, Florida, California, Arizona were for starters. Peter even took the four of us to Hawaii and I wound up climbing the Great Wall of China. To the outside world, my life was perfect. Something to envy.

It had only been two years since my mom passed away. Two years since I found my adoption papers. And one year since I learned that my birth mother had not died when I was born. That she handed me to my father. I still couldn't understand why a birth mother would hand a baby to the father. It's always the woman who accepts the baby into her arms. Why would my aunt tell me that?

Although I knew the chance was slim, I hung on to the hope that the woman who gave me life might still be alive. I had to try to find her. Armed with only a last name, I started with phonebooks. I checked out every phone book I could get my hands on, beginning with the local White Pages in my kitchen. I was on a mission. Each time I left the house, I scoured the area for telephone books. I looked everywhere. I found worn out directories under pay phones, in public phone booths on street corners, inside grocery stores and restaurants, outside gas stations. I even searched the filthy, torn phone books outside public restrooms and at airports. I couldn't find any Stambergs listed in the Cleveland area, or any other area in Ohio. As I traveled I continued my research.

After a short engagement, I gave in and splurged on a formal gown for the fairytale-like wedding of Peter's dreams. Yes, my fiancée hated that his mother-in-law controlled his first wedding and wanted ours to be perfect, his way, to make up for the past. All of Peter's friends, family and business associates, as well as my small family, attended the over-the top, seven-piece-band, catered extravaganza that was suddenly moved, due to an unexpected storm, from the garden to the family room of his uncle's Tudor mansion. So much for my request that the second wedding for the both of us remain simple. Being a trooper, I went with the flow, ignoring my migraine that began well before I learned about the valet parking and stretch limo he hired to take us to the Airport Sheraton.

It had been a long day. By the time the limo pulled up in front of our hotel, I was exhausted, on my third round of Advil, and dying to collapse in bed. Unfortunately, the clerk at the front desk insisted my new husband had not made a reservation. Finally, after producing evidence of our confirmation number, we were escorted to the honeymoon suite, which just happened to have a bottle of champagne on ice waiting, with our names on it. No reservation? Things were not going well at all. Since it was definitely too late to change our plans about the wedding day, I went with the flow. Finally in bed, I, thankfully, dozed off immediately.

San Francisco was our first stop before Hawaii. After checking in at our hotel and being escorted by the bellhop to our luxurious room, I was beginning to get excited about the next part of my life. I gazed out the window with child-like enthusiasm, hoping to catch a glimpse of a familiar sight. Perhaps the Golden Gate Bridge. "Don't unpack anything. We're not staying here," my new husband announced.

"Why?"

"Can't you see? This place is a toilet." It looked fine to me. I kept quiet. While Peter phoned the front desk to complain about our honeymoon room, I took the opportunity to check out the phone book, hoping to find someone who might share my birth name. Nothing, of course. No Stambergs in the entire San Francisco area.

As we continued to travel, I repeated the same process in all the hotels I stayed at. The San Diego Marriott phone book, no luck. The Phoenician in Phoenix? No Stamberg. I even looked up my birth name on our trips to Hong Kong and Beijing. Where do these people live? There must have been some Stambergs in New Jersey at one time because that's where I was born. Are any of them living there now?

Because the Internet was in its infancy at the time, I did most of my research in person. While tagging along on Peter's business trips, I played detective, scouring each ragged phone book next to the bible in every nightstand I could find. No luck. Stamberg was definitely not a common name. I finally had some success in New York, New Jersey and Florida. Taking advantage of the hotel notepads available in the desk drawer, I jotted down each complete name and address I found and secured them in my wallet.

After selling Mom's house, I left a few bits and pieces, mostly breakables that I didn't have time to properly pack, in my Aunt and Uncle's basement. When Peter and I moved into a new house, I was finally ready to have these items professionally boxed and shipped to me.

I watched as the UPS drivers unloaded the boxes from the truck, transforming our living room into a warehouse filled with my childhood memories, waiting to be rediscovered. I knew Mom's fancy schmancy gold trimmed Herend Hungarian porcelain that my dad shipped from Europe during the war, my inheritance, professionally packed in bubble wrap, was somewhere in this corrugated jungle. I was anxious to return each piece to its rightful place in Mom's breakfront.

After the brown truck drove away, I pulled up a chair to Mom's dining room table, wondering if I would always think of this as my mother's table. For the first time I noticed how Mom's slightly worn china cabinet seemed oddly out of place against my elegantly papered, colonial-style dining room wall, instead of that seventies-style flocked wallpaper backdrop I'd grown to love. Nothing felt right.

The stack of boxes was overwhelming. Since I felt no immediate need to unpack, I decided I'd open each box at my leisure.

After a few not-so-subtle hints from Peter, I realized I could no longer ignore the boxes piled in our living room. I needed to get to work sorting through my past. It was exciting. Like discovering Mom's ice cream spoon next to the basement freezer, the deeper I dug, the more I learned.

I never knew Mom saved Dad's letters from Europe during the war. And I found a tallis Dad had already bought for Brandon's future Bar Mitzvah. I had no idea that existed.

There was so much more. I found an entire box full of Dad's army medals and his dog tag. Opening one box at a time, I studied each scrap of paper as if I were preparing to submit them to the National Archives. I was determined to learn everything I could about my dad.

First of all, I had no idea he was such a romantic, signing each letter: Millions of kisses, hugs, pm-s, to you my dearest. Love, Andre. What were pm-s? PM as in nighttime? And I hadn't realized that Dad regularly sent money back home to his family during the war. However intriguing the cards and letters were, I put them aside when I came upon this yellowed, dog-eared, undated, newspaper article.

"Non-Coms Rate Salute in Hungarian Army; Discipline Stricter Than U.S."

If you think discipline is tough in the American army, drop in and have a talk with S-Sgt. Andre Perlmutter, supply sergeant of Co. L, 291st Infantry.

Sgt. Perlmutter served a year in the Hungarian army as a pre-OCS trainee.

"You wouldn't believe the extent of the discipline there unless you went though it yourself," he says. "We had to salute everyone of a higher rank than our own, including non-coms. And if a man failed to salute for some reason, the usual procedure was for the senior to make the junior walk in front of him twenty or thirty times, saluting each time."

"We were having a class on the machine gun one day on the fifth floor of one of the school buildings. During the course of the lecture, I said a few words to a buddy of mine sitting in the next chair. Unfortunately the non-com in charge of the class noticed it. As punishment, I was required to walk in a squatting position with hands on hips all the way to the basement."

The sergeant was a member of a pre-OCS battalion, made up entirely of college men. A graduate of a business college in Hungary, Perlmutter served his time in the Hungarian army in 1933-34. In the latter year he was attending the regular officer candidate course when his father died. Since the sergeant was the sole support of his family, he was released by the Hungarian army to return to civil life.

In 1937 Perlmutter came to this country and took as his first job the chore of dishwasher in a Newark,

New Jersey café. That lasted just ten days for by that time he had another job, this time in a Kearney, New Jersey butcher shop. Three years later he knew his trade and had saved sufficient money to buy a butcher shop concession in a super-market.

Inducted at Ft. Dix in 1942, Perlmutter was sent to the 314th Infantry of the 79th Division at Camp Blanding, Florida. From Blanding he was transferred to Camp Atterbury, Indiana to the 101st Infantry Battalion Separate. It was a unit composed entirely of foreign born GIs and included three members of the royal Austrian Hapsburg family. This unit was later split up by War Department order and Perlmutter was shipped as a corporal to the 75th Division.

Sgt. Perlmutter served for a time in the personnel section of the 291st finally becoming chief of the morning reports section. After being promoted to staff sergeant, he was transferred to Co. L where he is now supply sergeant.

You don't have to ask S-Sgt. Perlmutter which army and which government he prefers. You can tell by talking to him that when this one is over, he'll be heading back to the butcher shop in New Jersey.

According to the article, my dad served in the Hungarian Army before coming to the United States. I didn't know that. As a graduate of a business college, he was in officer's training, but had to leave because his father died. He needed to go home and take care of his family. I didn't know that. I didn't know any of this. Dad never talked about life in Hungary. He never mentioned his family. I didn't know his parents', my grandparents', names. Or his baby brother's name. Why should I? They had passed away years before I was born. I would never meet them anyway. It was almost as if he had not existed at all before he met, or I should say, married, my mom.

Whenever Dad mentioned the past, he talked about the

war. How he shopped during breaks from fighting for our country. At each yearly Seder, after finishing our requisite two-hour Haggadah reading (we read the entire book) in which our family took turns telling the story of the Exodus from Egypt, after we were finally allowed to enjoy Mom's matzo balls and a plate of gefilte fish, Dad would share his war stories, embellishing his shopping trips, telling how he'd run around Europe, buying Mom fur coats and brassieres, and his big coup, the Herend porcelain, my inheritance, that he had shipped from Hungary. *Was Sylvia having an affair with the UPS man?*, the neighbors wondered, as they noticed yet another brown truck pulling up to her apartment in Passaic, delivering, piece by piece, the set of dishes we used for every holiday. Our dinnerware, now my dinnerware, could very well be the largest assortment of hand painted Herend porcelain, outside of European aristocracy.

I knew enough about WWII to understand if we weren't laughing at Dad's war stories, we'd be crying at the atrocities. Like episodes of *Hogan's Heroes*, Dad sometimes recalled how the American soldiers would swoop in and steal swords and pistols out from under the passed-out or dead Nazis. Other than that, my dad shopped.

Until I read Dad's letters to Mom, I only knew a few things about the family that remained in Hungary. I knew I had one aunt who survived the camps and married a gentile. I knew Dad had another sister who lived close by, though we rarely saw them. I didn't know why, although I felt Mom didn't want them in our lives. Having been adopted, I figured they weren't related to me anyway. They weren't my blood. I didn't care. My dad didn't talk about them and I didn't ask questions. I didn't even include any of these people on the family tree I made in grade school.

We always hung out with Mom's family. Mom's friends. I never asked why Dad's sisters and their families weren't at our Seders, never came to my birthdays. They were, however, at our house once for a "family reunion" and my first wedding. I wonder how my father talked Mom into letting them come.

I found Mom and Dad's marriage certificate in one of the boxes. Married to Mom on October 19, 1941, it wasn't long before Dad was drafted into the US Army. I hadn't realized he was drafted before he was even a US citizen.

It took me quite a while to weed through the letters and telegrams that Mom had saved. I scattered the papers across my bed, sorting them into piles. Letters, cards, telegrams. There was far too much information to absorb at once.

I quickly began to understand that while my dad was off fighting a war, it was my mom's job to make sure Dad's family in Hungary had enough money to live on until he could get them out of Europe. Out of harm's way. He was trying to keep them alive.

As many of the pages, some of which were handwritten on transparent onion skin paper, were already faded and tearing apart at the folded seams, I was careful to handle each document gently, as if I were a museum curator.

The more I read, the more I appreciated my dad. I never knew how hard he had worked to help his family as they struggled to survive in war-torn Hungary.

S/SGT. ANDRE PERLMUTTER, 32 590 325
HQ. CO. HQ. DET. CAMP PHILADELPHIA
APO. 513. c/o PM.
N.Y.C. N.Y.
30 October 1945

Dearest darling Sylvia!

It looks like you'll have to buy some more stationary, because the 60 pointers will not leave the ETO before December or if I'm lucky than the end of November.

I put in for another furlough to Hungary. I could (have) asked for one to Switzerland, but it's better if I could go and see my sister again.

I took some pictures of my father's grave. (As)

soon as I receive them I shall send (them) to you. The grave wasn't in the best shape. I told Irenke to have it fixed and have a stone-wall made around the grave.

There weren't any letters here for me from you. I was hoping so. Your last letter was written on the 3'd of this month. I'm sure you wrote to me since. The mail situation is all mixed up. So many guys are being transferred in and out to this outfit daily, that it's no wonder. I talked to the mail clerk here and he told me it might take a whole month (for) the mail to catch up with the individual. So if you don't mind, send me one letter a week registered. According to him, that will reach me in no time.

In your next letter (registered mail) please answer these following questions, even if you've already answered them. First of all, how many money orders did you receive from me in the last month. And how many packages did you receive. I sent quite a few of them. One was sent to Mother. For you I sent about 8, I'm not sure. Let me see. 1. Two China vases. 2. Two water paintings. 3. Many small presents and a stamp collection. 4. Two German helmets. 5. I can't remember, but I'm sure I sent something else. Oh, yes, my three dimension photo. I sent you… about 15 or 16 money orders. In one letter was about 602.00 dollars and in the other one was 260.00 dollars.

Dad sent Mom eight packages? China vases, water paintings, German helmets? And almost one thousand dollars? That was a lot of money. How could he afford that?

Do not send any money to Irenke, because the exchange rate is very small. Did you send any money to Lili? If you didn't please send her $100.00.

Darling I guess I give you too much trouble with my relatives, but they need help badly. They've got to get out of Europe, because the situation isn't any better at all. I hope you don't mind.

Tomorrow I'm going to work in the P.X. I don't know now just what I'm going to do there. I'm sure it's a good deal. First of all it's better than any other jobs. And in the PX you could get many things – I mean if you are working there – that you can't get any other way.

Dearest I love you more than ever. You're probably tired reading in every letter that how much I love you, but I can't help I'm crazy about you. And I can't wait until I see you. I miss you terribly. O.G. is a very good boy. He misses his Sylvia neni too. Boy what I wouldn't give for a good kiss and a supper dupper PM session, but I guess I just have to wait.

Millions of kisses, hugs, pm-s, to you my dearest.
Love Andre

While my dad was serving our country, he was taking care of his family. It makes me think of all the service men in our country, putting their lives at risk every day, while still caring for and worrying about, their loved ones at home. But Dad's loved ones were the same people our army was fighting to save. It wasn't enough he and other US soldiers were trying to save millions from systematic destruction by the Nazi regime; my dad was trying to support his family and get them the hell out of Hungary. Before it was too late. He needed my mom's help. I wish I had her letters to him.

S/SGT ANDRE PERLMUTTER
c/o. PM. N.Y.C.N.Y
Camp Philadelphia, 14 November 1945

Dearest darling Sylvia!
Finally a letter from you dearest, after a whole month of silence. It's about time. All this time I thought it was the lousy Army Postal Service we have

here. I was wrong. It wasn't the APO's fault. It was my honey, who loves me so much and just got tired of writing to me. Took time out, for thirty-two days. I sure didn't deserve it. You should know better than that. If I was transferred my mail would reach me eventually. I should be angry at you and not write for a month and see how you would like it. But I love you too much and I wouldn't hurt you for anything in the world so you see you better make up and write me twice a day at least for a month to make up. To make sure you will not have any trouble getting any stamps, I sent you 25 books of 6 cent Air Mail (stamps). I guess it's a pretty smart way getting money home.

Why didn't she write to him for a whole month? Was she tired of taking care of his family?

Mailed you a package, with only a few things in it. Two bottles of Chanel No. 46, two porcelain ash trays, and a three piece sets of pottery souvenirs from Brussels. A tripod for our good camera. I bought a very good camera in Hungary.

Even though Dad was upset, he still sent her gifts.

Now I'll try to answer your questions. My sister Irenke is living with my Mother's brother Jeno and his wife. He was in Budapest. That's how he managed to (stay) alive. It seems that all the countries were cleaned first from the Jews. They started on Budapest, thank God a little too late, but they suffered enough too. They were rounded up and taken away to concentration camps. Lots of them were pushed with a machine gun to the Danube River. Now about our relatives In Budapest: My late Father's brother Jeno and his wife died from starvation. All Jews were taken to a Ghetto for only a half hour so they could buy some food. By the time they got there everything was sold out, so they couldn't get anything at all. Lots of them died from hunger.

Next Dad listed all his relatives that died in concentration camps.

In other words, all men over 45 and women, either pregnant or with a child 15 years or under, didn't come back at all. And all those that came back, no one could believe what they really (went through). All the girls had to be naked all winter long. The best they (could hope for) was to keep a shirt on. No shoes. In knee deep snow, pushing heavy carts. All the girls were tattooed on their left arm. I just don't want to tell you all those horrible things what they went thru. I could go on all night.

Oh my God. He's listing these deaths right after he talked about the gifts he bought. I can see the tears in his eyes. This war was personal. Dad lost most of his family.

It's no use sending anything to Irenke, because in Hungary she could buy everything she wants. I took her to Budapest and bought everything she needed. If you can, please send some clothing to Lillian. She would appreciate it.

I was glad to read that you have an apartment. The only trouble is that it's only three rooms.

I'm glad that you liked my three dimensional photo. It's not so good. You should see some good ones. They are really beautiful. I also sent you two lovely water paintings. Did you receive that? I sent you many packages. I hope they all arrive. Some of them have many nice things in it.

Wire me if you received the fur coat. I wonder if I paid too much for it. It cost me 560.00 with good old

American dollars. With the blue fox collar. Please let me know how much it would cost that home. Dearest I could of bought you a Persian lamb coat for 350.00. It was very nice also, but for my honey I bought the best. It doesn't get any better.

Wrote to Fred. He is in the same concentration camp where they burned my dear Mother. Imre was there also so I asked him if it is possible to find out what happened to him. Someone saw Imre after liberation. So there is a chance he might be in Sweden or Switzerland. Maybe you could inquire in New York about him. They have many offices.

It's getting late so I'll close my love letter. I still love you very much and miss you terrible. Soon as I can I'll be home.

Millions of kisses, hugs, PM-s to you
Andre

When I first began reading Dad's letters to Mom, I couldn't help laughing at his unique writing "style". Dad hadn't been in the country very long and his mastery of the English language was far from perfect. Trying to picture in my mind a very manly Zsa Zsa Gabor, I continued on. The more I read, the more I understood that the reality of war and the life of soldiers living far from their families, facing life and death situations in between shopping and posing for portraits, was far more complex than anything I'd imagined while munching popcorn in front of the TV watching those old black and white newsreels.

Dad mentioned that Mom liked a three-dimensional portrait. I remember that picture. It was the cool sepia-toned photo of Dad in full uniform. Hanging on our TV room wall, his eyes seemed to follow me wherever I went, as if I was in a funhouse. Creepy.

Dad was apologizing for causing Mom trouble with his relatives. Could this be when her resentment started? Mom was put in charge of making sure Dad's sisters got money. That his sisters got into the country and that they achieved citizenship. Was there enough money left for Mom to live on? Did my mother sacrifice her standard of living to take care of Dad's family? I don't know. But I sure envied his love for her. "I'm crazy about you!" Didn't that make it worth any sacrifices she might have made? I wanted to be loved like that.

Reading Dad's letter, dated November 14, 1945, for the first time, I wondered why he was still in the army after the war had ended. I guess the soldiers didn't automatically start marching home the minute Japan surrendered in September, 1945. I became angry at Mom for not writing for thirty-two days. Dad even sent her Chanel perfume and stamps. Was she mad at him?

After enjoying reading lighthearted tales of shopping excursions for furs and perfume, Dad's abrupt firsthand account of Holocaust atrocities took me by surprise. Even when I know I'm watching a movie, a fictional dramatization, like Spielberg's *Schindler's List*, I always turn my back, or at least avert my eyes from the screen to avoid watching those scenes in which skeletal bodies are piled high in the death camps. This depiction of Dad's family being rounded up and taken away to concentration camps, *pushed into the Danube River, dying of starvation, naked in the snow… no shoes… I could go on all night* ….is real.

No wonder my father never wanted to talk about the war. No wonder he rarely mentioned his family. When your past involves death and destruction, sometimes it's best to tuck away the memories and pretend they never happened.

I stopped and reread the paragraph about Dad's mother and brother. *…in the same concentration camp where they burned my dear Mother. Imre* (Dad's brother) *was there also…someone saw Imre after liberation. So there is a chance he might be in Sweden or Switzerland.*

Dad had told me his mother and brother were killed by the Nazis. He said they were shot to death in front of their house. That's what I always believed. Why would he make up that version? And, why was the "shot in front of the house story" so much easier for me to accept than knowing Dad's mother was killed in a concentration camp? Now, instead of picturing Dad's family living at home up until their time of death, I'm imagining my dad fighting a war to protect our country and our freedoms, yet unable to do anything to help his own mother, his family, from being systematically tortured and murdered. It all seems too real now. Why didn't he say anything? Was it too painful? Was he keeping the truth from me so I wouldn't ask any more questions? I'll never know.

I carefully stacked the letters and placed them in a manila envelope. I placed the manila envelope in the bottom drawer in my dad's desk.

After selling both of our houses, Peter and I were now living in a new house, our first home together. I picked it out. It was huge. Not by Hollywood, old money, or even new money standards, but to me, this was my dream home. Growing up, having to constantly travel clear across the length of our modest three-bedroom ranch to use the toilet, I fantasized of the day when I'd have my own bathroom. This house not only had a master bath, it had a Jacuzzi. Yes, I'd died and went to heaven. Peter teased me that I talked him into a quarter-million-dollar tub. That's ok. We could afford it. Besides, it provided Brandon and Katie with new rooms they could set up and call their own.

The two of us were determined to put our past lives, and marriages, in the past, where they belonged. With our traveling so much, my new husband encouraged me to cut back on my Weight Watchers meetings. Actually, he didn't want me to work at all. I didn't want to give up my meetings. Being a Weight Watchers leader not only gave me a chance to help others lose weight, it helped me keep my weight off. More importantly though, the part Peter didn't understand, my meetings, my working, gave me an identity of my own. I didn't want to just be someone's wife. Perhaps I had too much of an identity.

While traveling with Peter, I was always asked the same question, "What do you do?" Answering, "I teach Weight

Watchers" often thrust me in the limelight. It seemed like everyone I met was either a lifetime member or confessed to me that they "should get back on track". It became increasingly evident my husband did not like when I became the center of attention, especially since they were his business trips we were on. So I agreed to cut back. Since he wanted me home at night, making it clear he felt uncomfortable being alone with my kids, I dropped my evening and weekend meetings.

With less time out of the house working, down to only three or four meetings a week, I had plenty of time to sort through the remaining boxes piled up in the living room. Hefting one box at a time into the bedroom, I'd scour the contents, analyzing each and every item I came across. Reminiscing. There were so many pictures. I didn't recall ever seeing any of these albums, each one filled with black and white images of strangers. Each photo told a story of a happier time, before the war broke out. I carefully turned each one over, hoping to find handwritten clues to the subjects on the back. Other than a few Hungarian words sprinkled haphazardly throughout, the photos were mostly unmarked, providing me with no hint who any of these people were, except my dad. I'd recognize that face anywhere, at any age. With or without hair, he resembled Fred Astaire. I wondered who that cute girl was standing next to him. Undoubtedly another mystery.

Determined to start emptying the boxes, I dug down deep, pulling everything out, scattering a lifetime of history, my parent's history, memories, all over my king sized bed. Underneath the albums I found a few framed pictures.

I propped up the framed, three-dimensional portrait, the one mentioned in Dad's letter to Mom, against my grasscloth-papered wall. It seemed out of place there. As I pushed myself off the bed, stretching my cramped legs, I stared into my dad's eyes. Taking a few steps to the side, I noticed how the eyes followed me as they had years ago, when I had looked at the photo for comfort after his death. Walking backwards toward the bed again, the eyes kept their lock, holding my attention, telling me there's more in the box. Keep looking.

One photo in particular captured my attention. It was a small portrait of my dad, professionally framed with a red oval mat. With a full head of hair, this black and white picture must have been his high school senior portrait. Brandon had just brought home his high school portrait. I returned the albums to the box, for the time being, moved the three-dimensional photo to my dresser to hang at a later time, and carried Dad's high school portrait downstairs, placing it on the fireplace mantel on the opposite side of Brandon's portrait. It looked nice there.

I never enjoyed going out "on the town" for New Year's Eve. Having been married to an alcoholic, I learned in my Al-Anon meetings that this holiday was referred to as "amateurs' night": the one night of the year when non-drinkers, people who weren't used to regularly downing a six-pack before their morning commute, would get drunk and forget how to navigate a vehicle. Therefore, during my first marriage, we normally stayed home where we were safe. Not only safe from drunks on the road, but safe from fighting over his constant denial he had a drinking problem.

Since marrying a man whose birthday was on New Year's Eve, we always *had* to do something. I understood from early on in our relationship that spending any special event, even a weekend together, just the two of us, was never an option. Peter always needed a crowd. I didn't mind when he made the plans. However, his birthday was different. He expected me to make all the arrangements.

Luckily, I got off fairly easy that year. Instead of having to schlep downtown in the snow to the annual New Year's gala at the Renaissance Cleveland Hotel, or fend off crowds at an overpriced restaurant with a special limited holiday menu, I was given the ok to prepare a festive meal at home. I invited the company over for dinner. Just a few close friends sharing a bottle of champagne and the fresh (live) lobsters, one for each of us, Peter had shipped in from New England. Although much too rich (expensive) for my blood, I bit my tongue, reminding myself that since Peter earned the money, it's not my business.

I must admit this New Year's was actually a fun evening. I pretended I was Annie Hall to Peter's Woody Allen character as I cautiously grabbed the slimy, snappy crustaceans, their huge claws tightly pinned with large rubber bands, and tossed them in my largest soup pot filled with boiling water. The lobster dinner was so much easier when served to us already prepared at the Legal Seafood restaurant in Boston. But we did it right. With the nut crackers Peter bought for everyone, and the bibs I picked up at the party store, I'd say my New England dinner was a success.

After all the dishes were cleared from the table, I sent Peter and our four guests to the family room so I could enjoy a few moments to myself. After rinsing the dishes and placing them in the dishwasher, I took a deep breath and mentally prepared myself for the second part of the evening. From the kitchen, I turned out the lights and made a grand presentation of my famous, homemade cheesecake. It was a hit, as usual. After the candles were blown out, and Happy Birthday was sung, we all settled down on the white leather sofa. Turning on the TV, we waited for Dick Clark to begin his annual countdown to the New Year.

Finally relaxing for the first time all evening, I reached for my well-deserved glass of wine and propped my feet on the marble coffee table.

"I love that picture of Brandon. He looks so handsome." My friend Sophie said to me. She always had something nice to say about everyone.

I glanced in the direction of the photo. "Thank you," I chuckled, remembering our argument about his hair. Growing up in the 60's, I preferred my son with long hair. "He wanted to buzz his hair but I made him wait until after his senior picture was taken."

"Not that picture," Sophie said. "That new one." She was pointing to the red-matted picture I'd just placed on the other side of the mantel.

"Oh that?" I laughed. "That's not Brandon. That's a picture of my dad. I just put it there."

I met Sophie through Peter. She is the greatest person. Being a realtor, she made her living collecting friends as others collect recipes, most likely in the hope they would call her when they want to sell their home. As a matter of fact, it was Sophie who helped me find my new home. However, Sophie was different from most of the people I've known. She was genuine. The real deal. If she paid a compliment, I believed she was sincere. I trusted her. I enjoyed spending time with her and her family.

But I'd never confided in her about having been married to an addict and she didn't know that I was adopted. And why should she? These topics just don't pop up in everyday conversation. I always thought it was funny how people who didn't know my story were always telling me I looked like my dad. That's not what she was telling me.

"It may be your dad, but it looks exactly like Brandon," Sophie insisted.

I looked over at the mantel. Dad's photo was on one side; Brandon's was on the other. I set my wine glass down on a coaster, stood up and walked over to the fireplace. I removed the vase from the middle of the mantel and placed it on one of the built-in shelves. I returned to the fireplace, picked up both of the photos, my dad's 5"X7" black and white and Brandon's 5"X7" color portrait, and placed them side by side. All six of us gathered around the picture.

You could hear a pin drop as everyone stood still, ignoring Dick Clark in the background. We were staring and analyzing both pictures. It was true. The eyes, the ears, the mouth, even the hairline was the same. Since Brandon had brushed his hair straight back for the photo and Dad had a full head of hair at the time, they sported the same hair style. *Oh my God*, I thought, *these pictures are almost identical. They could be the same person.* "If I didn't know better..." I stopped talking. I didn't want to go into my life story now. There will be time for that another day. Right now, I thought, why shouldn't our guests assume my son would look like his grandfather? There's nothing strange about that. But there was.

I couldn't sleep that night, tossing and turning, for the first time wondering if my dad could possibly have been my birth father. It would make what my aunt said make sense. "Your birth mother handed you to your father," my Aunt told me. Why would a birth mother hand a baby to the father? They always hand the baby to the mother. It's the mother who always wants a child. It's always the mother who is the driving force in an adoption. Why would my birth mother hand me to my father unless my father is, or might be, my birth father? Is that possible?

I'd waited so long to find out any information about my birth. Ever since I realized it took two people to have a baby, a man and a woman, I started wondering what happened to my birth father. It was too much of a coincidence that he would have died before I was born as well. Sometimes I tried to convince myself that they both died in a car accident and I was miraculously born alive, unharmed. But the fact that my birth mother handed me to anyone meant that she must have been alive when I was born. At least for a short while.

And how many times did I assume my birth was the result of a rape? That a tragic, violent act brought about my life was so upsetting, I'd immediately dismiss this theory. But it would be a valid reason to give away a child. Who would want to spend a lifetime staring in the face of a constant reminder of a brutal attack?

My father, looking like my son, invites so many questions, and few answers. Is this a new puzzle piece in the mystery of my life? Is it even possible? I wish someone was alive who could answer my questions. Seeing these two portraits, two almost identical 5"X7" photos taken over sixty years apart, was unnerving.

I set out, determined to learn the truth. With the souvenir desktop copier I had left over from my business with Ryan, I made dozens of black and white copies of each picture, enlarging some, shrinking others. Some pictures I left whole, other copies I cut out, tracing the outline of the head, the ears, the eyes onto a blank sheet of paper like those silhouette drawings they sell at amusement parks. Then I'd take the cutouts of my dad's picture and Brandon's and paste them side by side on a blank piece of paper, the original "cut and paste" method that we used years ago.

After spreading all the images on a table, I began to analyze each picture, each tracing. On one hand, I knew the idea of my dad being my biological father was far-fetched. Ridiculous. Impossible. Why wouldn't Mom and Dad have told me? But, if it was true, if there was the slightest possibility my dad was really my birth father, I wanted to know. I wanted to know the story. I needed to know the truth. But how could this happen? Did anyone else know? Those people who said I looked like my dad. Did they know something?

It was January and Peter had finally returned to work. The few Weight Watchers meetings I had left were packed, since everyone makes a New Year's resolution to lose weight. In between my meetings, I obsessed over those pictures. Jotting down the facts I knew about my dad, I started searching for additional information about him and comparing my findings to Brandon. I compared their height, weight, eye color, blood types.

On our new computer, I researched genetics, specifically eye color. Dad had hazel eyes. My children both have hazel eyes. What are the odds of my children having hazel eyes when their dad has hazel eyes but I have brown eyes? It looked to me like my brown eyes were a dominant color. The way I read this information, I probably would need to have someone in my bloodline with hazel eyes for both of my children to have inherited hazel eyes instead of my brown eyes. It was just a theory. I didn't really understand the research that well.

I called my friend for help. "Sophie, your son is a doctor. Would you mind if I ask him about the odds of me having brown eyes and both my children having hazel eyes?" By this time, since she knew my whole story anyway, I would not hesitate to follow any path that could help me learn my background. With both of my parents passed away, I wasn't worried about hurting anyone's feelings. Divulging anyone's secrets.

"Of course!" Sophie answered. "David's coming over for dinner Sunday. How about you and Peter come over around 5?"

By the time Sunday evening arrived, I was anxious to get to the purpose of our dinner. I wanted to jump right in and hit Dr. David with my research. I wanted to shove my photos in his face, and wait for his response. For his verdict. For his expert opinion on whether I had a case. That my dad could actually be my father. But I needed to wait. I needed patience. I needed to politely eat Sophie's dinner, make pleasant conversation and enjoy the dessert she bought from Davis Bakery before approaching her son. Finally, the dishes were cleared and the coffee was served. It was show time. I approached Sophie's "son the doctor", explained my hazel vs. brown eye theory, and handed him one of the black and white copies I made showing both my dad and son.

"Let me see the picture of your dad," David said. I was confused. Couldn't he see I had just handed him photos of two people printed on one sheet of paper.

"You have the picture of my dad. And the picture of Brandon." I told him.

"There must be a mistake," Doctor David said. "You gave me two pictures of the same person. I need to look at the picture of your dad to compare."

He turned the piece of paper over that I handed to him, scrunching his eyebrows as if I was pulling his leg. Or, maybe he thought I didn't realize I copied the same picture twice. Only I hadn't made a mistake. I realized at that moment, at a quick glance, it did look like the two images were the same person, wearing two different sets of clothing.

"No," I told David. "The two pictures on this piece of paper are two different people."

We looked at each other, convinced there's definitely more to my adoption than I was told. Sophie refilled our cups of coffee and we sat down at the kitchen table to discuss the possibilities. Sophie was so much more than my new friend. She sold my house and Peter's house in addition to helping us purchase the new home we were living in. I was realizing that she might just have hit on discovering the most significant puzzle piece of my life. I was beginning to believe I just might be able to figure out my background.

With this one piece of my puzzle, I believed there was a good chance I was related, somehow, to my dad. The fact that he looked so much like Brandon, and his eye color was the same as both of my children, were facts I could not dismiss. Dr. David agreed there is a good chance I possess a recessive gene for hazel eyes in order for my children to have both inherited their dad's hazel eyes, rather than my dominant brown eyes. I needed to figure out where this piece fit in the jigsaw of my life. Could this have been why my mom didn't want me to know anything? She didn't want me to know that I was somehow related to my dad, and not to her? I was determined more than ever to learn as much as possible. There must be more clues.

I pulled Mom's lock box from my dresser drawer and brought it over to my bed, along with a fresh legal pad and pen. I settled into a comfortable, cross-legged position, and pulled out my adoption papers, this time studying them as if I had stumbled upon a rare Civil War document that I was examining for authenticity.

I titled the first page of my legal pad: Adoption, Female Baby Stamberg. Under this heading I started jotting down notes, pretending I was standing at a whiteboard in a corporate brainstorming session. *Come on guys. Give me ideas. Don't be afraid. There's no right, no wrong. No one's going to judge you.* OK, no one's going to judge me. I tend to be too hard on myself. *I'm going to throw ideas out.* I'd glanced at this document before, but never studied it. I'd never taken it line by line, looking for clues. Now's the time.

The first thing that caught my eye was the method of adoption. Mine was a private adoption, with an attorney who, I'm sure, passed away years ago. Since there was no agency involved, there would be no one I could contact. No elderly social worker would be hanging on to her job, waiting for my call, so she could fulfill the promise she made to my birthmother so many years before. Yes, I'm sure there is no one sitting at a rotted-out wooden desk, squinting under a flickering fluorescent light, periodically touching the worn-out, frayed file in her cabinet, the one holding the dog eared note, the loving, heartfelt message from mother to daughter explaining how she would always love her darling daughter, but for now, this is best.

My adoption was private. I went to my computer and searched the attorney's name who handled my case. Yes, I was right. He died a long time ago. I'm sure my files have all been shredded. I needed to move on. Still in brainstorming mode, I jotted down additional questions.

Why would they have had a private adoption? Why wouldn't they have just gone to an agency if they wanted a baby?

Why is there no father's name listed? Was the father unknown? And why was the birth mother's name spelled two ways? Stamberg/Stomberg. I noticed that the first time I'd looked at the document and I still couldn't figure out why they did that. They had to know the correct spelling of the name. It's a legal document. They should have checked the spelling before typing it up. Maybe the secretary couldn't read someone's handwriting. Or was Stamberg the mother and Stomberg the father? That doesn't make sense. I'd been searching both names in the telephone directories, but it's still weird.

Other information: Union County Court. Born in Newark, NJ.

I've tried to get a copy of my original birth certificate, but New Jersey won't give me one. It's sealed. Permanently. They will only give me the one that was revised, a year after my adoption.

All I really had was what appeared to be my birthmother's name. That's not much to go by. I didn't know if she was single or married when I was born. She might have been married and got a divorce after she found out she was pregnant. If her name had changed, I worried I might already have hit a dead end.

That kind of thinking wouldn't get me anywhere. I needed to find some family member who remembers something. Anything.

Going back to: *no birth father's name*. What about the pictures? The picture of my dad and Brandon. Maybe that's why there wasn't a father's name listed. My birth mother was protecting his identity. He asked not to be mentioned. Because he was married. If the "he" was my dad, what was my dad doing having a baby with another woman when he was married to my mother? Did Mom know about this? Did she agree? Maybe they were divorced for a few years and got back together. No, that doesn't make sense. I was getting ahead of myself. I went back to my photo albums. I rooted through the old pictures of my dad when he was younger, and me, growing up. I pulled out some pictures, spreading them across my bed, arranging them in lines and columns, like I was playing the game *Concentration*, trying to match photos of my dad and me.

I'm not sure if it was true, or if it was my over-active imagination, but the more I looked, the more I found pictures that seemed to match. At five, I'm sitting on my daddy's lap. We shared the same shape face. The same smile. Again, as a teen, standing next to Dad, there it was again, I'm noticing similarities. I can definitely see how others said I looked like my dad. Is this enough information to assume that he is my father? Maybe he had a relative that I don't know about who could be my birth father. Someone who looks, or looked, like him. Someone I never met. Maybe someone who had already died. Maybe he was my birth father and that's why I looked like my dad. I don't know. I gathered all the pictures of me and Dad. Then I went through the pictures of Brandon and Dad. Once again, I noticed the same bone structure, the same ears. I gathered the pictures and carefully placed them in a red, commemorative Oreo tin that I couldn't throw away after the Oreos were finished. Opening the tin every once in a while, I'd stare, examine, and wonder why Brandon and I resembled my dad so much when I was adopted.

CHAPTER ELEVEN

By 1997, the Internet was growing by leaps and bounds, offering free access to more and more information. I began scouring the web every day hoping to find any clue to my history. Initially, I searched adoption sites where birth mothers could register their names, hoping to finally connect with the children they put up for adoption years before. Unfortunately, no one was looking for me. Before long, I broadened my search away from adoption sites. Combing the entire web, I hoped to connect with anyone who shared my birth name. Soon my persistence paid off with a meaningful hit.

Entering the name "Stamberg" in the Yahoo search engine, I found a site, the Social Security Death Index, which listed dozens of Stambergs. I was hoping one of these people on the list, although they were already dead, might somehow be connected to my birth mother. I didn't have a clue what the relationship would be, but since the Stamberg name wasn't very common, I believed I was on the right track. Perhaps, someone, somewhere, would know something about my existence. I prayed I would not find my birth mother's name on the list. That would mean she had already died. However, in reality, with just a last name, how would I even know if I had found my birth mother?

I tried to keep optimistic. Remembering my aunt had said my birth mother was "an older woman", I assumed she was not a typical pregnant teenager when I was born. But "older" could have meant thirty. Or maybe forty? Since my Aunt was twenty six when I was born, anyone older than twenty six could have seemed like an older woman to her.

Scanning through the list of names, Joseph, Irving, Yetta, Sara, Max, Herman, Rose, I'm strangely comforted by the Jewishness. All my life my dad drummed into my head the importance of my faith. "Don't ever forget you're Jewish," Dad said on my wedding day. He never knew how I had always wondered if I was Jewish by birth, or if I was raised Jewish because I was adopted into a Jewish family. My relief at learning of my Jewish heritage was overwhelming. For the first time, I felt like I belonged. I felt part of a group. All those years in Temple, wondering if I was just there because my dad was forcing his beliefs on me, I now know that I am Jewish by birth. A member of the tribe. Those Hebrews that wandered around the desert for forty years really were my ancestors. Instantly, my life took on a new meaning.

The Social Security Death Index, in addition to listing the name and date of death, listed the birth date and the last residence. When opening up several records I noticed the record also listed in which state the person's Social Security number was issued. Many of the Stambergs received their Social Security numbers in New Jersey and later moved, retired, to Florida, where they died. I printed out the list of names and began highlighting those who had lived in New Jersey. Maybe I could look up their obituaries online. Maybe that would help me find more names to search.

I was getting frustrated. My AOL dialup was so slow. And every time the phone rang I got booted off. But I kept up my search, going back and forth to the kitchen for another glass of Diet Coke, or some cookies, while I waited for my computer to connect again.

Continuing my research, I remained focused on two geographic areas: New Jersey and Florida. I looked for names and addresses of potential contacts: living Stambergs who might know something about family members who resided in New Jersey in the 1950s. One name popped up repeatedly: Jack Stamberg from Pembroke Pines, Florida. Mr. Jack Stamberg was a regular contributor of "letters to the editor" of a local Florida newspaper. And he was very active in the Jewish community. This man, obviously a caring, community minded individual, just might know something, or at least lead me in the right direction. Give me a starting point for my search. If nothing else, unlike the names listed in the Social Security Death Index, Jack Stamberg was alive.

It was time to start my long awaited mail campaign. I felt good that I could finally put my college degree in marketing to use. I started composing a form letter, explaining that I was adopted at birth and I was looking for information that would help me find my birth mother. I didn't want to scare anyone away by allowing them think I had ulterior motives. I needed for them to know I didn't want money. And I wouldn't intrude on their lives. I just wanted to know who I was.

Initially, I would send my letter to all the names and addresses I'd collected and saved from various telephone directories over the years. And, of course, to my new Internet contact, Mr. Jack Stamberg. I made dozens of copies of the best picture of me I had; the one Brandon took when I reached my Weight Watchers goal. With my bright smile, hair perfectly coifed, and posed at my piano, who wouldn't be proud to have me as part of their family? I planned to include this image in my mass mailing, along with a brief note asking for any possible information about my birth.

I sat down to my computer and composed my letter.

Dear ___ Stamberg,

My name is Joan. I was born in 1954 in New Jersey. I don't want to interfere with anyone's life, but I am trying to find out who my birth mother is. My

adoption papers list her last name as Stamberg. I have enclosed a picture of me. If I look like anyone in your family, or if you have any information about a baby born in 1954 and put up for adoption, please let me know. Thank you so much for your help.
Sincerely, etc.

Then I included all my contact information.

I was right. I knew I struck gold when I found Jack Stamberg online. Although he didn't address my adoption, or mention knowing anything about my birth family, he did respond to my letter. Almost immediately. Without asking any further questions, most likely assuming I was a family member doing research on my lineage, Jack sent me a list of all the original family members, including the brothers, their business, and their Jewish connection.

The list seemed endless. With such a large, and according to Jack's notes, closely knit clan, it was amazing to me that I had had such little success searching phone books. Maybe all of them were in Florida or New Jersey. Could the people on this list really be my blood relatives, I wondered? It seemed to me like all the Stambergs are related. If that's the case, how would I ever figure out which Stamberg could be my birth mother?

Not knowing what to do with the list Jack sent me, I carefully folded the letter, placed it back in the envelope, and inserted it in a brand new manila folder that I labeled "Adoption". I then placed the folder next to my Oreo box filled with pictures, to be revisited, and obsessed about later. There were still many letters out there with my picture in it. Maybe someone would actually recognize me. Maybe someone would think I looked just like one of their family members.

Most days my mailbox was stuffed with bills. Cleveland Electric Illuminating Company, Cablevision. All the bills arrived in very distinctive envelopes that I tossed directly into my bill drawer, to be dealt with later. Junk mail in flashy envelopes touting a life changing event awaiting me if I responded NOW went in the trash. This handwritten note was different.

My hand began trembling as I carefully opened an envelope that was most likely addressed by a grade school teacher. The perfect penmanship reminded me how at one time I used to have a beautiful handwriting. I even won a handwriting contest in the fifth grade. I stared at the open envelope, afraid to see what was inside. What if this letter contained information about my birth mother? I was excited and nervous at the same time. My palms actually began to sweat. I needed to sit down.

I took the envelope to the family room. Before removing the letter, I lowered myself onto my couch, curling my legs beneath me. I wanted to get comfortable before I read what was inside. What if it was someone telling me to leave their family alone? I couldn't blame them for that. I put the envelope down on the coffee table, padded into the kitchen, stared in the refrigerator, pulled out a Diet Coke bottle, poured myself a full glass, then returned to the family room, settling onto the couch again. I took a sip of my soda, placed the glass on the coffee table and removed the letter.

Elaine called herself the Stamberg family historian. Seriously? Who has a family historian? Who has a family large enough to have designated someone to keep records of the family? I grew up hiding in my room trying to ignore my mother yelling at me. My dad worked late every night. I wouldn't want anyone documenting that. Family? OK, I had cousins who lived next door. And my dad had sisters that my mom apparently didn't like. We never talked about our history. As a matter of fact, in my small family we hardly talked about anything other than the fact that my room was messy and I used too much ketchup, ruining my mom's chicken. And frankly, I doubt my cousins thought about us at all. They were busy leading their own lives. Now I'm discovering I might have been born into a family special enough to have a historian. Cool!

I started communicating with Elaine Stamberg Bloomberg in 1998. She wasn't the one who received my introductory letter. She had been forwarded my letter from another family member. Since she obviously knew everything about the family, and was therefore, the most likely the person who could help me, I wrote back to her, outlining my story. This time I provided more details than I had in my original mass mailing.

February 24, 1998

Dear Elaine,

Thank you so much for answering my letter. I really hope you can help me find my roots.

I want you to know that I do not wish to intrude on anyone's life; I'm just seeking answers to questions I have been asking my whole life.

I'll give you all the background information I have. I was born in August 1954 in New Jersey and immediately adopted. All of my life my mother told me (when I begged for information) that my birthmother died during childbirth. After my mother died in 1988 my aunt told me my birthmother didn't die during my birth, that when my parents went to pick me up at the hospital, my birthmother handed me to my father. Now I know there was a woman that gave birth to me who might still be alive.

While I was going through all of my parents documents (my father died in 1983) to handle their estate, I found my adoption papers. I was adopted in Elizabeth, Union county, New Jersey, through a private attorney. My birth name was Female Baby Stamberg. This is when my search began. I started looking for the name Stamberg in phone books as I traveled and found the name was not very common. It was not until I had access to the Internet that I was able to find a number of Stambergs that I could contact.

(On the adoption papers the name was listed as Stamberg/Stomberg but my research indicated the Stambergs seemed to be the ones living in Northern

NJ at that time.)

The addresses on the Internet are not very current and the contacts I made were encouraging but I eventually reached a dead end.

Whenever I tried to put the idea on the back burner I'm once again reminded of my adoption. When I go to a doctor they ask for my family medical history. I have to tell them I'm adopted and I don't have a medical history because NJ is one of the few states remaining that hasn't unsealed birth records for adoptees over 21 years of age.

I stopped my search until an event occurred that was impossible for me to ignore. Last year I received a box of old photos that had been stored in my cousin's basement. Some of the pictures were framed and I displayed them. Friends seeing one of the pictures remarked, "That's such a nice picture of Brandon," my son. When my husband and I examined the photos, we discovered that my father (adoptive father) was the exact double of my son. We looked at photos of them both at different ages and the resemblance was uncanny. After showing the photos to a private investigator and a doctor, we were told that there seems to be a 99% chance that my adoptive father, Andre Perlmutter, was actually my birth father.

This is where my curiosity was peaked again. We hear so many adoption stories where someone finds out their parents aren't really their parents and they wish to meet their biological parents. My story is the opposite. I think my adoptive father was actually my biological father and was unable to tell me. It would also provide answers to why my mother wouldn't talk about (my birth) and actually lied to me.

Since I know a Stamberg woman that lived in NJ in 1954 gave birth to me, I'd be very interested to learn what the story was. Was it a love story, but my birth mother was already married and her husband couldn't accept her "love child"? Or was it a story of surrogacy where a woman helped out my father to give him a child that he so desperately wanted? (I have letters from him to my mother in the 1940s where he writes about how much he wanted a baby and he was 43 when I was born.) Or was my birth mother single and alone? Whatever the story was, if someone knows I would be very anxious to learn the story.

I would be so thankful if someone could help me find my roots and put the puzzle pieces together.

There's a good chance that the Stamberg in question might have passed away by now. But if she did, I hope she didn't take the story with her. Any information you could give me would be greatly appreciated.

Again, Elaine, I don't want to cause problems or upset anyone's life. But surely, if you were in my situation, you would be just as interested. Even if you would just be able to get vital medical information for me, that would be helpful.

By the way, I grew up in Lake Hiawatha (Parsippany) New Jersey. My father owned a store in Irvington. I am married and have two children, Katie, 20 and Brandon 21. I also just became a grandmother in January. I hope you can help me. Thank you very much for your time.

Sincerely,

Joan

I didn't know what to expect after sending off that letter. Maybe this woman was just given my name so she, as the "historian", could tell me in her official capacity to "go away", to "leave their family alone". Or worse, she might come back with "how dare you accuse someone in our family of having a baby out of wedlock?" Even if she did tell me to go away, just knowing I connected with a "Stamberg" felt like an accomplishment. My search was successful. I found someone who shares my birth name. That means something.

Although I was anxious to hear back from Elaine, life went on. I was busy enjoying my new granddaughter, Sammi. Katie, exhausted after giving birth, was nervous and hadn't a clue what to do with an infant. I knew just how she felt. All my high school babysitting experience didn't help me in the least when I found myself alone for the first time with my son, a miniature human being, totally dependent on me for everything. There was no waiting until "the parents got home" to be relieved of my TV watching and M&M eating duty.

Caring for Brandon had been, at times, challenging. Not only was I a new, young, mother, I was a new, young, mother of a child with special needs. Just giving him a bath was difficult. I needed to make sure the corrective cast for his clubfoot stayed dry. To do that meant wrapping his leg in a plastic bag before I bathed him in the sink. He didn't like that procedure at all. However, that was nothing compared to the inner strength I had to summon up every time we left the house. It was hard for me to ignore the accusatory glares from passers-by, staring at my baby's casted leg, silently implying I had hurt my child. Assuming that his leg was broken, and I was negligent. I broke his leg. Yes, I take full responsibility for the cast my puppy, Koko, wore after I dropped her on the hard, tiled, basement floor when I was ten years old. But my child being in a cast was different. I would never let anything or anyone harm my precious baby.

Cradling my perfect granddaughter in my arms was different than holding either of my own babies. I was comfortable, at ease, and in heaven. Inhaling her warmth, I had to remind myself she wasn't mine to keep. Only to borrow. After placing this perfect infant into the crib Peter and I set up for her in our home, I took pictures. Lots of pictures. I couldn't stop looking at baby Samantha, this new person with my bloodline.

I know how to count my blessings. It was important to me

to be able to stay home and care for my children until they were old enough to go to school. Again, I enjoyed the luxury of staying at home to care for my granddaughter while Katie returned to work. We made a deal. I would take care of Sammi while Katie worked, provided she enrolled in school, with the goal of getting a degree of her choice. She chose nursing. School would start soon.

Katie worked her ass off. At six o'clock every morning, Katie drove a sleeping Sammi over to our house, placed her into her crib and left for work. My day started when Sammi woke up. I'd change her, feed her, bathe her and put her down for a nap. Then I'd take a nap until Sammi woke up. Again, I'd feed her and change her. Then I'd photograph her. Just as I had photographed baby Brandon and baby Katie, I couldn't get enough pictures of my granddaughter. I was in heaven. Exhausted, but happy.

I was more than happy. I was obsessed with showing off my beautiful granddaughter. Figuring it was more socially acceptable to boast about a grandchild then one's own children, I'd foist my pictures on anyone who was within range. Everywhere I went I carried around a purse-sized photo album as if I was preparing to submit head shots to the Ford Modeling Agency.

Even if Sammi was with me in her stroller, I'd still show my pictures. "I can see how beautiful your granddaughter is," they'd say, no doubt mentally patting me on the head, hoping I'd go away. "No, look at these pictures." I'd counter. "She looks even better in these shots. See her cute outfit…" Yes, I was obnoxious. But, having the most beautiful granddaughter in the world, I wanted, needed, everyone to know that.

What they didn't know, what I kept to myself, was how much I thought Sammi looked like Brandon and Katie. And me. Standing in line at the Toys R Us, Acme, Heinen's, wherever, the clerk, thinking Sammi was my daughter, would invariably look at my granddaughter and remark, "You look just like your mommy." Yes, I was a very young grandma. Yes, it confused Sammi at times. But I never minded the mix up. All those years growing up, longing to look like someone, I now had three people who look like me.

Sammi's afternoon naptime became my obsessing time. Settling in with a cup of strong coffee on my nightstand, I'd spread out Sammi's pictures on my bed and line each one up alongside photos of Brandon and Katie at the same age. Again, I'd play my version of *Concentration*. I'd find a picture of Sammi that looked just like a picture of Brandon. Then I'd place the two images next to each other. Then I'd match up a photo of Sammi that looked just like Katie as a baby. Next I'd compare these pictures to my baby pictures. Like a complicated jigsaw puzzle, some of the pieces were beginning to come together. I couldn't see the entire picture yet, but what I had was a good start. A good start to learning more about myself.

Looking at the spread of photos on my bed, I started to appreciate the value of my existence. I always wanted to know how I came to be. I wanted to know if I was a love child. If I was wanted. Or, if I was the product of rape, the idea that disturbed me the most. The thought of being born due to an act of violence was unthinkable. Matching up Brandon's picture with my dad's, I thankfully have ruled out the possibility of my being the product of rape. My dad was a gentle, loving man. The type of man who would well up during heartwarming McDonald's commercials. I was still trying to get used to the possibility that my dad was also my birth father.

I have two beautiful, healthy, brilliant children. My daughter has a child. No matter what the circumstance of my birth was, this was my legacy. These remarkable human beings exist because one woman, one woman who I do not know, who I may never know, had the courage to give birth to me. To give me life. And because of my life, others are on this earth. This all became my *It's a Wonderful Life* story and I played Jimmy Stewart's role. I decided that, regardless of what I might learn, if anything, about my adoption, I felt blessed to be alive.

I pulled out the Oreo box again. I took out my stash of pictures and lined up my baby photos alongside Sammi's, Brandon's, Katie's and my dad's. Yes, I definitely saw a similarity. I noticed the cowlick in my baby photo. I recalled Katie, as a teen, trying to wear her hair with bangs, unsuccessfully, because of her cowlick. I noticed Sammi has a swirl at her hairline, certainly the beginning of a cowlick. I looked at my dad's and Brandon's photos, side by side. As children, they both sported curly blond locks. Yes, I realized, I do have relatives.

I started to wonder if my birth mother had other children. I might have a sister. Or a brother. They could look like me. Maybe they had a cowlick that they hated. Sometimes I wished I wasn't so consumed with what most people take for granted. Like when I was married to an addict, this was definitely something I must deal with alone. It's something I couldn't talk to anyone about. They'd think I was crazy.

CHAPTER TWELVE

March 2, 1998

Dear Joan,

  I was happy to hear from you and hope that I can be of assistance in your search. I was eleven in 1954 so am not as aware of what was going on in my family as an older person might be. I did speak with my parents in Florida, however, and got a little information. As of this point, there is absolutely nothing conclusive, but I will share with you the little I could get.

  First of all, let me tell you a little about the Stambergs. The original siblings came from Poland in the early 1900's. My grandfather settled in Brooklyn with his wife (who bore him seven children – six boys and a girl). The six Stamberg boys all wound up in northern New Jersey...one in Teaneck, four in Bloomfield, and one in Irvington. All six brothers were in the shoe business. The one in Teaneck had his own store. The other five had two stores – one in

Bloomfield and one in Irvington. Only one of the original Stamberg children is alive – my dad, the youngest, who lives in Tamarac, Florida and who received your original letter. The other two Stambergs in Florida are a surviving sister-in-law and a cousin. There are distant cousins in Illinois whose last name is Stomberg, probably due to a spelling error on Ellis Island. The six brothers had a majority of daughters so most of us cousins do not have Stamberg surnames any longer, hence your difficulty in locating them.

I asked my parents if the name Perlmutter rang any bells. They recall that my uncle did have a friend named Perlmutter, but they believe it was Louis. I plan on asking the cousin but think I should do it in person, not over the telephone, in case I am on to something. The Stamberg cousins continue to be a very close knit group (as were the brothers) and I don't want to cause any estrangement. I do, however, plan to pursue it for you. I have the "Family Album" with all the birthdates (and death dates) of the family. I looked up the ages of aunts and cousins since you believe your birth mother is the Stamberg. The aunts were all in their forties in 1954 and the cousins were mostly in their late teens. My parents insist that there is no way any of them could have been pregnant without their knowing as there were "Stamberg Family Circle" meetings every month. It is obviously more logical that the father is the Stamberg...but you seem pretty sure that your adoptive father is your biological father, right? Could a friend of the Stambergs given birth and used the Stamberg name? Why won't New Jersey let you see your birth certificate? Are there any of your aunts and uncles alive who may know something? Why won't they tell you now that both of your parents are deceased? I empathize with you for the need for some kind of closure regarding your birth.

The picture you enclosed with the original letter

does not reveal any Stamberg resemblance. Remember, however, that if one of my aunts is your birth mother then she is not a blood Stamberg.

Do you know what kind of business you dad had in Irvington? Did he commute there from Lake Hiawatha, where you mentioned you grew up? Maybe some more information will jog my parents' memories. Right now, this is about all I know to share with you. As I mentioned earlier, I will present this to the cousin who grew up in Irvington to see if she is aware of anything, but I want to do it in person so it will have to wait until I can go to New Jersey. I've discussed this in depth with my sister (who is five years my junior). She and I believe Irvington is the link. Therefore, we believe this cousin (who was sixteen in 1954) may be the link. My sister and I are romantics. We want to help you. Our folks said to basically, "let it go"...but we can't do that to you.

Look forward to hearing from you again. Mazel Tov on becoming a grandmother...so young.

Sincerely,
Elaine Bloomberg

OK, it was Elaine's dad who received my letter. I don't think he is the Jack I wrote to, since Jack already answered me. Elaine talks about the Stombergs. They are the same family, just a different spelling of the name, most likely changed when they arrived on Ellis Island. That's what I thought, that there were two branches to the same family. That, however, doesn't explain why both spellings would be on my adoption papers. You'd think an attorney writing up a legal document, or his secretary, would check the spelling for accuracy.

What's very interesting is that one brother lives in Irvington, where my dad had a store. Coincidence? I don't know right now. But it's definitely worth pursuing.

I find it a little troubling that Elaine wonders if a friend could have used the Stamberg name. If that's true, I'd most likely never learn anything about my birth. I'd have reached a dead end. Once again, I'd think for a legal document, such as adoption papers, the attorney would check out the name for accuracy. Both in spelling, and to make sure the client was who she claimed to be. This was not a situation like we have today in which anyone can go to an office supply store, or online, pick out a legal form, and type whatever name they want on the document. Besides, a notary public would insist on seeing proper identification.

In order to keep on pursuing my history, finding out who my birth mother was, I need to make some basic assumptions. The first being, I need to trust that the lawyer got the woman's name correct. That the woman named in the document was indeed my birth mother. I have no choice.

Elaine asked about my dad's business. I will give her as much information as I can. And I'm glad she's going to share my information with the "Irvington" connection. That's a very good start.

I must boast I was a great mom to Katie while she was pregnant. Not only did I support my daughter financially and emotionally, I also fed her, stocking up on her favorite ice cream flavors and Little Debbie Nutty Bars. At dinnertime, I was more than willing to whip up my homemade lasagna at the drop of a hat. In other words, having been pregnant myself and understanding the psychological and physical needs of an expectant mother, I helped satisfy each and every one of my daughter's cravings, making the ultimate sacrifice of snacking along with her.

I knew I shouldn't have quit teaching Weight Watchers for Peter. I just got tired of him always complaining when I wasn't home. And I got upset when he wouldn't even come home for dinner if I wasn't there. I'd had enough fighting during my first marriage. I'd do anything to keep the peace. Therefore, I gave up all my meetings. Besides, I rationalized, my daughter needed me.

Unfortunately, while Katie packed on about fifty pounds of baby weight; I gained more weight than the average father-to-be puts on during his wife's pregnancy. I couldn't let my daughter eat alone, could I? After Katie gave birth, she just resumed her normal "pre-pregnancy diet" and her excess pounds melted off quickly. That was not the case for me. There's no such thing as "normal eating" in my life. I'm either on a diet or off. I needed to take more drastic measures to get back on track.

After Sammi was born and she was my responsibility while Katie was at work, I had to find daytime activities to keep us occupied. We weren't going to stay home all day watching Sesame Street or playing with baby toys, I needed to get out of the house. Since I'd gained so much weight, I knew just where I belonged. I needed to return to Weight Watchers as a member to drop my "baby weight."

Pushing a stroller into the meeting room, I noticed members smiling at me, thinking that I had every right to gain weight at this "special" time of my life. Little did they know that I was the codependent, not the mom. Weight Watchers was easier for me this time. I was motivated to lose the weight quickly. I was sick and tired of having to re-stitch the seams on my black stretch leggings almost daily, having nothing else that fit me since Katie gave birth. Not only was it frustrating having to start over, my "fat jeans", my largest jeans that I wore the first time I joined Weight Watchers years before, the ones I'd saved as an incentive to never gain my weight back, were too tight.

Standing in line at the Hudson Weight Watchers center, I didn't know whether to laugh or cry when people thought Sammi, sound asleep in her stroller during my meeting, was my own baby. Feeling so old and round, I found it sadly laughable that anyone would think I could actually get pregnant. Who could possibly be attracted to me looking so bloated? Besides, I certainly wasn't going to tell anyone that my marriage, my second marriage, the one I was determined to make work, was crashing fast. Maybe it started to go downhill when we tried to start a family of our own, but found it impossible. When the tests showed I was fertile and he wasn't, his behavior towards me began to change. Failure wasn't easy for Peter to swallow. Maybe that's why he wanted me to quit working. Maybe being the bread winner made him feel better about himself. Who knows? All I know is I was determined to get back in shape as quickly as possible. I followed the new points program to perfection, dropping the extra pounds in no time.

My days babysitting were becoming long. Sometimes, seeming endless. Sammi, still coming to the house at six in the morning, no longer fell back to sleep. She cried, summoning me into her room to start my day before the crack of dawn. Sometimes she refused to take a nap, choosing instead to be cute all day, demanding I video her every move. From the first time she lifted her head off her infant seat, gazing with delight as she glanced around the room, instead of just staring at the ceiling, to her attempts to climb upon the piano bench and create music, I captured her on tape. I was convinced she was a genius after noticing how she surpassed every milestone in the book, "What to Expect the First Year".

I continued photographing my granddaughter, not resting until Katie got home and we relaxed for an hour of *All My Children*, before she took her daughter home to her apartment.

Now, in addition to my photo puzzle obsession, Sammi's naptime turned into web surfing time. With the Internet growing by leaps and bounds during the late 1990s, each time I Googled Stamberg, I got more hits.

One day, again typing "Stamberg" in the Social Security Death Index, insanely hoping for different results, my heart raced as I noticed a listing I hadn't seen before. My hands started trembling as I noticed, for the first time, right on the same screen I'd stared at so many times, the page I'd printed on numerous occasions, right there in black and white, my birth name. And my middle name. Next to each other. I quickly wiped my sweaty palms on my jeans before pressing the "print" function on my computer, needing to make sure I didn't lose this information. There it was. Right before my eyes. "Ella

Stamberg." My middle name, Ella, right next to my birth mother's name, Stamberg. This was too much of a coincidence to ignore. Ella was not that common a name.

I clicked on her highlighted name link to read more about this woman. This Ella Stamberg. I learned, although she died in Florida, she had lived in New Jersey. I was born in New Jersey. Then I noticed that, although many of the "Stambergs" lived in New Jersey at one time, almost all of them had a "last residence" in Florida.

It did not take me long to leap to conclusions, working out the entire scenario of my existence in my head. My dad's store, Andre's Meat Market, was on Lyons Ave. in Irvington, NJ. Maybe Ella was one of the Stambergs who lived in Irvington. Dad's store was a butcher shop, actually, a small grocery store. The only grocery store in town. He offered *free delivery service*. I pictured this woman coming in to Dad's store to shop for groceries. Nothing out of the ordinary there. I noticed from the social security death index that she was close to Dad's age. Two years younger, actually. My dad was charming. At parties, he flirted shamelessly with the women, calling each one "doll". I was never sure if he used the word as a term of endearment, or because he didn't couldn't remember the women's names. That didn't matter to me. In my mind, I pictured a scene straight out of *Guys and Dolls*, only instead of small-time gangsters playing craps in an alley, my mind placed the scene in a butcher shop, complete with dancing girls and boys in the background doing high kicks on the glass-enclosed meat cases.

I pictured this woman bringing her basket of groceries to the counter in the rear of the store. They struck up a conversation ending with my dad pointing to the sign on his door offering "Free Delivery". She agrees. He asks for her name and address, promising to have her order ready for delivery right after he closes the store, around six o'clock. "My name is Ella..."

I never knew my dad's mother's name was Ella until I started reading his letters. Another secret. Why would they keep it from me that I was named after my grandmother? Mom and Dad only talked about an "Aunt Ella". Now, armed with the knowledge that there was an Ella Stamberg and my father's mother's name was Ella, I'm picturing my dad's eyes tearing up at the mention of his mother's name. The woman who gave him life, who he could not save from the Nazi's. I'm sure he delivered her groceries. Maybe a lot more than that.

I started seriously wondering if this woman, Ella Stamberg, could be my birth mother. Did both of my parents agree my middle name would be Ella as a tribute to her, or Dad's mother? Or, possibly, could Dad have insisted my middle name be Ella as a way for me to find her someday?

Now I'm thinking about my mother, Sylvia. The woman who raised me. The woman who wanted me to dye my hair to look like hers. The woman who fought with me tooth and nail when I didn't agree with her, hating my independence. Hating that I had my own personality, a personality that was so different than hers.

I wonder if Mom knew my birth mother. If she had ever met her. If she did meet her, did I look like her? Was my dad cheating on my mother with this other woman? Did Mom see this woman's face in my face? Is this why she told me my birth mother died in child birth? Was this her secret? Is this why she hated me? Because I was a daily reminder of the other woman, the woman my dad had a baby with when my mother couldn't give birth? Was I a constant reminder of my dad's betrayal every day of my life? Did my mere existence cause Mom pain? Seeing me every day, knowing how I came to be, must have been so agonizing for her, no matter what the story was. The more I learn, the more questions I have. I need to ask Elaine.

I write to Elaine again, this time asking her about Ella, giving her my theory.

March 7, 1998
Dear Elaine,

Thank you so much again for answering my letter.

I'm glad you and your sister are romantics. Again, I don't want anything. My husband and I are very comfortable. I just have a large empty space from not knowing my roots. I will try to answer the questions you brought up and give you information from my search so far.

The "Irvington Connection":
Adoption Papers: Female Baby Stamberg (Stomberg)
State of NJ, Union County
My father's business: Andre's Meat Market, 751 Lyons Ave. Irvington, NJ. A small grocery store.
My family lived in Union, NJ (Stuyvesant Village) until 1956.

When I found out my birth mother was still alive when I was born, my aunt indicated that she was an "older woman". When I asked her recently for more information since I found the pictures (of my dad), she denied knowing anything. I think even if she did know my father could have been my birth father, she probably would not know the "real" story because my parents would have made up a story they could live with (just as they made up a story to me).

I'm enclosing pictures to show you why I'm almost sure Andre was my birthfather. Look at the resemblance between Brandon and Andre. All their features are almost identical and I was always told I looked like my father.

Now, if my birth mother was "older", my guess would be that she would have been in her late 30's or early 40's. Andre was 43 when I was born. I don't know about the surviving sisters but I was wondering if you could find out about Ella Stamberg. She died in 1989 and would have been two years younger than Andre. And she lived in Northern, NJ. Why Ella? Her age is close enough for them to have been "friends" and my middle name happens to be Ella. Coincidence? Maybe. And, there are many surprise pregnancies in the 40's because people don't expect it to happen. She might have been married and her husband wouldn't accept the baby. I'm thinking your cousin that was sixteen in 1954, her mother could be a possibility.

I trust you will be discreet when asking about this because I don't want to destroy anyone by letting out their secret. But my whole life, even though I loved my small family (I was an only child), I never had any blood relatives. I married and had my children very young because I wanted a family of my own. I love my children more than life itself and whenever people remark how they look like me I'm thrilled.

I do feel incomplete not knowing my birth family and I think it's so nice of you to be so helpful. I always wondered if I had siblings. I didn't leave my phone number before or ask for yours because I didn't want to intrude if I wasn't welcome. I'm giving you my phone number now, in case you want to contact me with questions or information.

Once again, I thank you and your sister. I look forward to hearing from you.

Sincerely,
Joan

I can't wait to hear what she has to say about Ella. There are too many coincidences to ignore. I can't get the picture out of my mind. A woman walks into my dad's store. Nothing unusual about that. He offers to deliver her groceries. He does that all the time. He takes out his order form, preparing to write down the woman's name and address. She says, "Ella. My name is Ella Stamberg."

My dad glances up from his note pad. "Ella? Did you say your name is Ella?"

The woman placing the order senses something is wrong. She sees the man's eyes tearing.

"I'm sorry," my dad says to her. "My mother's name was Ella." I imagine Dad telling this stranger, the stranger with the same name as his mother, how she died. How he tried, but couldn't save her. What better way to strike up a conversation? Did this conversation lead to a friendship? Maybe more? I need to learn more about Ella. I hope Elaine has some answers.

March 13, 1998

Dear Joan,

Your latest letter contained a lot of information which I shared with my parents and sister. My parents still contend that a friend of the Stambergs must have used their name. My sister and I continue to believe that it is not possible to do such a thing with legal documents, such as birth certificates or adoption papers.

The little bit of background I have is as follows:

Elaine goes on to list members of the Stamberg family and their history.

As far as my cousins go, the oldest girls were in their teens in 1954 and my mom insists none of them could possibly have been pregnant...so it would have been one of the sisters-in-law. That would fit your "older woman" theory as some of my aunts were in their late 30's or early 40's. How did you get the name Ella Stamberg? She was my aunt. She was a super, special lady. The coincidence of you sharing that name "blows me away", but it is too eerie to be true...especially if you consider the fact that your parents never chose to discuss the issue...If this was the case, why would they include your birthmother's name into your name and be forever reminded? Doesn't make sense.

I agree with you that the resemblance between Brandon and Andre is uncanny. I tried to visualize you as a Stamberg, however, and could not pick up any resemblance to our family or any of the cousins. Your face, however, was in the fold of the letter and made clear scrutiny difficult! Do you have any other pictures of you that might reflect a Stamberg face? I will be in Florida in April and will bring the letter and pictures with me. Jack seems to be the historian. Perhaps he knows something else.

I still plan to share this with the cousins in New Jersey...but in person. I hope to see the cousins in May. Until then, I really don't know if anything I have said reveals any new information for you. I wish you good luck in your search. I can genuinely understand your need for some kind of closure. I am really curious as to how you know about Aunt Ella. Do you want to tell me? She lived in Irvington, NJ.

Wishing you the very best.
Sincerely,
Elaine

This was so exciting. Each day I sat by the window watching for the mailman like Koko used to stand guard waiting for my dad to come home from work. Only this time, it was not the mailman who interested me; it was the possibility of my life, my beginning, unfolding page by page, in an envelope with the return address: New Haven, Connecticut.

As soon as the mail truck disappeared down the street, I ran to the box, greedily searching for my treasure. Once found, I rushed to read the note, answering it immediately so I could keep our conversation going.

Elaine described Ella as a super special lady. Sharing the same name "blows me away." She lived in Irvington! Bingo. I must be on the right track. When Elaine questions them naming me Ella, a constant reminder, I wonder again if my mom knew about this woman. Maybe she just knew Dad had been unfaithful and didn't want any details. Ella was my dad's mother's name. Even if I wasn't my dad's blood, how could Mom deny him naming me after his beloved mother, who had died a tragic death? Besides, it's a Jewish tradition to name a child after a loved one who had passed away. Both of Mom's parents were still alive when I was born. I should have been named after my dad's mother. It's the "Joan" part that doesn't make sense. I finally realize that being named "Ella" makes perfect sense, regardless of my birthmother's name. I was named after my paternal grandmother.

I wish someone was still alive to tell me the truth. I know Mom and Dad had been trying for years to have a child. He said so in his letters, "looking forward to getting home from the war to start a family". I didn't see Mom's responses to the letters, but I knew my dad wanted a family. I know from my own marriage that not being able to have a child can cause stress on a relationship. Maybe they were fighting. Maybe Dad was threatening to leave her if she treated him badly. I certainly know her temper first hand. Maybe she was depressed and took it out on him. Maybe he found comfort in another woman's arms. I wish I knew more. Elaine is my only link to possible answers.

March 16, 1998

Dear Elaine,

That was so uncanny when you said Ella Stamberg lived in Irvington – another Irvington connection.

The first place to start genealogy research is the Social Security Death Index. It's on the Internet. It lists the place where the Social Security Number was issued and where the person died.

The Internet also lists names and an address of everyone listed in phone books but gives no other information. So what I did was simply look up Stambergs in the SSDI to see which ones had lived in NJ to narrow down the number of people I would contact by mail. I found many Stambergs who lived in NJ retired in Florida. So I sent mailings to names in Florida.

I also just received a brief letter from Jack in Pembroke Pines, and he knows some NY Stambergs. They are his cousins. He sent me a list of addresses and phone numbers. I'm not contacting them. I just followed up to Jack with a letter of explanation of my search like I did with you, to see if he knows anything.

Back to Ella. The first time I searched the SSDI the name Ella wasn't there. The birthdates didn't seem to have any meaning for a successful follow-up.

When I searched again the name Ella showed up. NJ; age close to my father's; and the name was the same as mine. I got that same strange feeling as I got when I started comparing the pictures of Brandon with Andre. I did "what ifs". What if she was carrying a baby that she wanted to keep but they decided the baby would be better off with Andre (perhaps her husband was away at war at the time.) She didn't want to let go but agreed to, under one condition, that I be named after her. Also, if she lived in Irvington, she almost must have gone to Andre's Meat Market at some point.

You asked if I had any other pictures that reflected a Stamberg face. When I was comparing pictures of Brandon and Andre I chose pictures of the same age and close to the same pose. I don't know what a Stamberg face looks like. I've never seen a picture of a Stamberg. If you had a family photo you could send me, I'd be happy to see if any of my photos

resemble cousins, aunts, etc. and send you one.
    I look forward to hearing from you. Thanks again.

Sincerely,
Joan

    I popped this letter right into the mail box, raised the red flag, and got back to life. I knew I couldn't spend all my waking hours obsessing about my past. There were things I needed to take care of right away. The number one item on my agenda, after taking care of Sammi, was me. I continued attending my Weight Watchers meetings, planning to go back to teaching as soon as I returned to my goal. I needed to plan a life for myself after Katie would no longer need for me to take care of Sammi. This babysitting gig was just temporary. Besides, I needed to think about my future. And possibly, a future without Peter.
    Still, I looked forward to hearing from Elaine. I loved how she called her Aunt Ella, her favorite aunt. She saw the resemblance between Brandon and my dad. She was on my side. With my marriage on the rocks, Elaine was my lifeline. Yes, another letter!

March 24, 1998

Dear Joan,

    Again, it was nice to hear from you. It is fascinating how you were able to get to the point at which you now find yourself in your search. I am not very literate with the computer and the Internet, so I find it mind-boggling. I'm pretty good with the word processor, but that's about it!
    I've been sharing your letters with my sister, and we continue to wish you good luck in your search. We certainly hope you find some closure. Right now, however, we really don't have much information to

share with you. Our parents are the remaining Stambergs (from this group of Stambergs), and they have no knowledge of any pregnancy in 1954. My Aunt Ella was a terrific, dynamic woman whose great love extended to all of her nieces and nephews as well as her own two children. She and my Uncle Hy displayed much devotion throughout their lives. She fits into the Irvington connection, having lived on Lyons Avenue, but it isn't logical to assume that she could be your birth mother. I will share the letters with her daughter when I see her in New Jersey and see if we come up with any ideas.

Meanwhile, I am visiting my parents in Florida in two weeks and will bring the pictures you sent to me.

There is a medical condition in the Stamberg family of which you should be aware. There has been a tendency toward latent diabetes (developing in later years). You are still young, but I thought you should know about it. Not everyone develops it, but it did exist in a few uncles and one cousin has it.

Wishing you good luck in your search. I genuinely hope you find some answers to your quest.

Sincerely,
Elaine

Ella lived on Lyons Avenue. The same street my dad's store was on. She had to have known him. She had to have shopped at his store. She was most likely there every week. She probably sent her children to pick up a few groceries, a loaf of bread, quart of milk, when she was too busy. Yes, I'm sure she knew my dad.

Elaine is going to share my information with Ella's daughter. I found Ella's obituary online and learned this daughter would have been sixteen years old when I was born. I know Ella also had a son who would have been about seven at the time of my birth. Could the sixteen year old possibly be my birth mother? The answer to that could only be yes if I wasn't guessing that my dad was my birth father. Since Dad was forty-three when I was born, there was no way he would have been with a sixteen year old girl. That's impossible. If I'm on the right track, and I think I am, Ella is most likely my birth mother.

CHAPTER THIRTEEN

By the time Sammi was four months old, I was back to my goal weight and teaching Weight Watchers three evenings a week. Now, when Katie would come to pick up Sammi after work, we'd watch *All My Children* together, after which I'd get dressed and head out to work. Having a purpose other than babysitting and housekeeping, my life took on new meaning.

It felt so good to fit into my old, small clothes. Out of my sweats, I'd admire myself in the mirror, amazed at how fast I'd transformed my appearance. My life. Caring about how I looked, I took the time to apply makeup. Fix my hair. Basically, my old job was waiting for me. All I had to do was place one phone call. When I dialed the toll-free telephone number on my membership book and explained to the new area manager I had taught Weight Watchers before, she had meetings ready for me. I was back. And better than ever. My members loved my story of feeding my pregnant daughter, gaining "baby" weight right along with her. Then, how I got right back on the horse, on track, and turned my life around. I was a positive example for others, and for myself. This time, no one would stop me from achieving my personal goals. Not only was I confident about my weight and career; I was starting to believe I might indeed learn my roots.

Unfortunately, my marriage was a different story. Living with Peter was becoming more unbearable with each passing day. I didn't want Katie or Brandon to know that my husband and I had been sleeping in separate rooms for months. Like I needed to stay married to Ryan until after I graduated from college, I not only hoped to be able to stay with Peter until Katie and Sammi no longer needed my help, I still looked forward to us starting a business together like we had planned to do for years. I prayed Peter's temper would improve after we had our own business instead of his having to spend his days at the job he'd grown to hate. The very well-paying job he'd grown to hate. Even though I thought we had agreed that Peter would keep working until we started our business, without warning, my husband abruptly quit his job. If I thought his episodes of rage were bad before, without Peter having an office to go to each day, our marriage continued to worsen. His anti-depressants did nothing to curb his fits of anger. And our attempts at counseling failed.

Thank God I had Elaine's letters to look forward to. After not hearing from her for months, I wrote to her again.

July 19, 1998

Dear Elaine,

I hope you are doing well. Since I haven't heard back from you after your trips to NJ and Florida, I'm assuming that either no one knows (or remembers) anything or people in your family are denying the possibility that someone in the family had a baby and put it up for adoption. I understand this. Most people would deny the possibility (even though) it happens so often, even to the "nicest people in the world" and to those very religious. My family denied that my father could have been my biological father saying that he was "so devoted to my mother". But when they saw the pictures they were dumbfounded. Even doctors have looked at the pictures and information I found and said that my son and my father looked so much alike they thought they were looking at the same person.

My parents have passed away so there is no one left to confirm or deny anything. You know that I was interested in learning about the story of my birth, not on intruding on someone that doesn't want to believe I exist. I really don't want to bother anyone if they do not want to be bothered.

I still have that void though. These are my options. I can go to court to try to unseal my birth records. Unfortunately NJ usually denies this. I can hire a private detective to investigate hospital records at the time of my birth. Or I can request a DNA test be done on a family member to determine if he or she is a relative. A child of my biological mother would be approximately a 25% match to me.

Elaine, I'm sure Ella Stamberg was the greatest woman in the world and I know you loved her. But you saw there were so many coincidences: her age, she lived in Irvington, she lived on Lyons Ave. Her name is the same as mine (why wouldn't my father have named me after his mother who died after being shot to death by the Nazis?) If it wasn't her and someone did lie on the adoption papers, someone must have been staying with her at that time and used her name. But if that were the case, why would I have her first name? Could she have gone away for a few months during the summer of 1954 so no one would have known her condition?

I haven't contacted anyone else in the family out of respect for you since you said you would do some family research for me. I'm asking you to please, find out if Ella's children would be willing to take a DNA test. I'd pay for it. It's a very simple blood test.

Also, I'd really appreciate it if you could send me a picture of her, anything when she was 50 years old or younger. I look very similar to my father, but I would very much appreciate the opportunity to see a picture for myself.

Please help me with this simple request. It is out of respect for the whole family that I am not contacting anyone else directly and asking upsetting questions.

Once again, thank you and I look forward to hearing from you.

Sincerely,
Joan

Elaine's next letter to me was short and blunt. Ella's daughter, Iris, told Elaine to "stop this nonsense." She wanted "no part of this charade"; insisting Ella could not possibly have had a child without her, being sixteen at the time, knowing it. "Drop it," Iris ordered.

For the first time, I truly understood the expression "my heart stopped" as I realized I might have come to the end of my journey. There was a distinct possibility that I would never find an answer to my question. I might never learn who my birth mother was. I might have to give up my search. I might have to admit defeat. Since I'd believed quitting was not an option, this was difficult to swallow.

After Ella's daughter ordered her to drop the subject, to pretend she'd never heard from me, I didn't expect to receive more mail from Elaine. I thought that chapter of my life had ended. Almost as if a part of me, the part that existed during the nine months before I was born, the pain and suffering a woman endured to give me life, was wiped out again. First, when New Jersey sealed my original birth certificate, then again, my accepting the end of my search for my birth mother.

It was time to go on with life. Put the past in the past.

I was floored the day I received a thicker-than-usual envelope in my mailbox containing a folded-up photocopy. Yes, the woman I'd come to know continued to try to help me. I always believed in my heart that if I saw a picture of my birth mother, I would know her. I would somehow recognize her face. We would connect on some sort of spiritual level. I knew this picture was exactly what I'd been hoping for, praying for, as long as I could remember.

I read Elaine's note telling me about the enclosed photo. As if I was holding a potential winning lottery ticket in my sweaty palms, I cautiously clutched the envelope containing a picture of the woman I already believed gave birth to me. In a way, it was like I had already won the lottery. I was hesitant, afraid, to remove the photocopy from the envelope and unfold it, not knowing what to expect. I quickly sorted the rest of the mail, putting aside the bills, throwing away the ads, and took the opened envelope with the photocopied picture up to my bedroom, locked the door, and sat on the bed, preparing to study the photo.

I often wondered if Ella looked like me. Would I look like her? Would I like what she looked like? Was she pretty? Or dowdy? I smiled, remembering what my Grandma looked like when I was growing up. Little, round, with light blue hair. I never cared what she looked like. I loved her with all my heart. And she loved me, totally. Would I even recognize someone who looked like me? How old would she be in this picture? I hesitated a moment before carefully unfolding the grainy black and white copy of an old photograph.

I smiled, noticing Elaine inserted an arrow pointing to a young, very attractive woman. Glancing at the other women in the photo, the woman with the arrow pointed in her direction was obviously the best dressed, classiest, prettiest woman in the group. I needed to take a better look. Immediately, I got off my bed and placed the photo in my scanner, enlarging the image so I could get a better look at this woman. The woman I might have been named after. I printed several copies, in various sizes, neatly folding the images and placing the original, for safekeeping, in the Oreo box. Another copy went into the photo album in my purse. The final copy remained on my dad's desk, open, so I could carefully analyze her face, her features.

Do I resemble this woman with the curly hair, I wondered, thinking about my own thin hair? I didn't know the answer to that question. But strangely, I couldn't shake the feeling my own eyes were staring back at me. I couldn't wait to show the picture to Peter when he got home. That was a disappointment.

September 17, 1998

Dear Elaine,

I just can't get over how nice you are to send me that picture. Words cannot express my appreciation for your kindness and caring. I didn't expect that, especially after receiving your letter saying that Ella's daughter says it's not possible. I don't blame her. Who knows, though, if my original letter had been forwarded to her, she might be the one trying to help me solve the mystery?

Ella was a beautiful woman. She looked full of life. I showed the picture to my husband and asked if he saw any resemblance. (He likes to tease me when I get carried away and would be the first person to tell me I was nuts if I was on the wrong track.) He looked at the picture and told me he saw some resemblance, bone structure and coloring perhaps, but he immediately said she's got the same smile as my daughter Katie. So I found a picture of Katie in a similar pose and compared them. I think if people saw Katie and Ella having lunch together they would assume the two were related in some way.

Did Ella have a sister, cousin, or relative that might have visited her during the winter of 1953/54?

That would have given us an Irvington/Lyons Ave. connection. She might have let a relative use her name. I also still believe the name on my adoption papers was the name of my birth mother because I was given up immediately at birth and in the 1950s; only the mother had to sign away rights to the child. The birth father usually played no role.

Anyway, Happy New Year to you and your family. You truly are a mensch!

Sincerely,
Joan

I didn't agree with Peter, as usual, but I didn't bother arguing. Instead I searched through my old albums and found a picture of me at the same age Ella was in the picture Elaine sent me. We were both posed the same way. I saw resemblances. I didn't just see Katie in Ella's face. I saw me. My eyes. My eyebrows. My jawline. Even our posture was the same. I was sure I'd found the right woman. Although the picture of Ella was small and grainy, I carried it with me at all times, staring at the image several times a day. The more I compared her image to my picture, the more alike we looked, in my mind. I couldn't stop thinking about this woman. Soon I felt like I knew Ella. Like she was a part of me.

I convinced myself it didn't matter what Ella's daughter said. It was possible that Iris's mother could be my birth mother. Iris was sixteen when I was born. I know sixteen-year-olds. They pay very little attention to their mothers. I spent my entire sixteenth year hiding in my room, coming out only at night, after I knew my parents had retired to the TV room. Like a pesky roach, I would scurry into the kitchen when the lights were off and the coast clear, grab some leftover Entenmann's cheese strudel and a handful of cookies, and run back into hiding before I was caught. My mother could have gained and lost thirty pounds during my teen years and I would never have noticed. I was too caught up in myself. Or, if I did notice, I would have assumed she was getting fat. Pregnancy would never have occurred to me.

As long as I was continuing my online research, I tried to find pictures of Ella's two children. I couldn't find any. I didn't really expect I would. I wondered if they looked like their mom. Or like me? I wouldn't ask Elaine for a picture of them. That would be going too far.

I hadn't heard from Elaine in a while. I really didn't know what to say to her, but she was my only connection to learning about my birthmother. I just needed to keep in touch. Maintain some sort of communication so she won't forget about me. I wrote another letter.

4/19/99

Dear Elaine,

I hope you are doing well. We are all fine here. I want to thank you for your continuing words of encouragement. I think I've reached a stalemate here. From my research, I'm still finding it impossible to open my original files. Even if I did, the files would still say "Stamberg" and I'm unaware of any other "Stambergs" living in that area at that time. So your cousin would still say the records were forged, or a wrong name was used. I might just let it rest unless I uncover more info.

I would love to meet you sometime and thank you in person. We are out your way occasionally for business and family visits.

Take care,
Sincerely,
Joan

Although I had basically let go, deciding to put my obsession behind me, move on with my life, I never stopped believing, hoping, that someday I'd find more information. With the original group photo of Ella tucked away in my Oreo box, I kept the enlargement I made in my purse, always close to me. Every once in a while, I'd take it out and carefully unfold the paper, now coming apart at the seams. I'd stare at her eyes, her posture, the curve of her smile, while looking at my reflection in my mirror, searching for similarities. Always analyzing, wondering, could this be my birth mother? If I had to give up a child, I know I would always think about them. I imagine my biological mother, or any mother, would feel the same way.

The next letter I got from Elaine surprised me.

September 28, 1999

Dear Joan,

    Did you hear the news! Tennessee just passed legislation to allow adopted adults to see their previously sealed records, and a few other states (they actually mentioned N.J.!!) are considering following suit! I thought of you immediately and became very hopeful for you!
    Wishing you good luck in your frustrating search. I think of you often. Hoping you will find closure, and peace soon.

With warmest wishes, Elaine
Perhaps this will be a good new year for you and your family! Hope so.

Elaine's kindness, her caring, totally overwhelmed me. Who the hell am I? A stranger who, out of the blue, tells her I might be related. Not only that, but I'm telling her I might be the illegitimate child of a woman she loved. A woman she admired. I'm opening up the possibility that her favorite aunt, not only cheated on her husband, Elaine's uncle, I'm saying this woman might have carried and given birth to another man's child. Yet, she never argued this point. She never accused me of sullying the woman's good name. She allowed my feelings. She considered my theory as a possibility. She passed no judgment, accepting the possibility that her aunt, for whatever her reason, whatever her circumstances, might have made a choice to give birth to a child and give it up for adoption. I never imagined it was possible for a total stranger to open her heart like that to someone she never met. She believed my story. She listened. I am so thankful that she took me seriously.

CHAPTER FOURTEEN

10/8/99

Dear Elaine,

    That was so nice that you would keep me in mind when you heard about the Tennessee legislation. I read about it in the Adoption Newsletter I receive by email each month. Maybe there's still hope for NJ. We'll see.

    I really do feel I have the answers I was searching for. My father seems to have been my "birth" father. (Both of my children resemble him so much). If the adoption papers said my birth mother's name was Stamberg, I'm sure my original birth certificate will also.

    My family is doing fabulous. My son Brandon is graduating from college in December. My husband is getting his MBA also. And my daughter, Katie, has started nursing school and she's doing great. I'm having the time of my life with my 21 month old granddaughter Sammi who talks non-stop. I'm working part-time "counseling" and my husband and I will be starting a new business this year.

Closure would be nice, but I do feel very satisfied that I learned so much from my own research.

Other than the adoption newsletter, we don't get much news here (in Ohio) about NJ. So, I really do appreciate you keeping me up to date about NJ news. Thank you and I look forward to hearing from you again. I also wish you and yours a happy new year.

Warmly,
Joan

Looking back on this letter I'm taken aback at how optimistic I sounded. Or should I say, what I good liar I was? I guess I got good practice constantly assuring my mom that my life was perfect, couldn't be better, despite the fact that I was living with an addict and spending my life running back and forth to AA meetings, halfway houses and rehabs. *Everything is great! I'm so happy!* I'm good at putting on a brave face. A façade.

I didn't need to burden Elaine with my reality, my anything but perfect life. She didn't need to know how exhausted I was each night. Being responsible for a toddler from six in the morning until Katie got home at four was draining. I was getting too old for this. I wanted to be the grandma. I wanted to enjoy my granddaughter, and let Katie do the work. It was confusing for Sammi as well. Strangers referred to me as her mommy, while I referred to Katie as Sammi's mommy. Soon, to Sammi, I was Grandma-mommy and Katie was Mommy-grandma.

I needed time for myself. I didn't feel guilty all those nights I handed Sammi over to Katie the minute she walked in the door so I could run out the door to teach my Weight Watchers class. Teaching was my lifeline to the outside world. And a way to earn a few bucks.

The money, although not much, was important to me since

I didn't know how long my marriage would last. And I earned enough working part time to pay for my daughter's education.

Since Peter quit his job and started lying around the house all day while I was trying to take care of a baby, he was in my way. My days were long and I was tired. If Peter wasn't going to offer me any help, I wished he would go away. But he didn't. Overcome with resentment, my fuse grew shorter each day.

Since I couldn't run and hide in the bedroom while I was taking care of Sammi, I found myself losing my temper. "Get your snoring ass out of the family room!" I demanded, frustrated and resentful watching him, unshowered and unshaven, curled up on the sectional like a pile of trash waiting for curbside pickup. "Can't you see I'm trying to take care of a baby? If you want to sleep, go to your room!" I ordered to deaf ears. Just the fact that he had his own room said more than my words did. I didn't resent that he had nothing to do all day as much as I resented that he did "nothing" in my way. I liked to play with the baby on that sectional. If he wasn't going to help, I didn't want him around. I didn't need two children to take care of.

It was sad, but taking care of Sammi made me count my blessings I didn't have a child with Peter, as I'd be raising it alone. *What happened to that charming man I married?* I wondered. *The one who used to dress up for our dates, selecting the perfect cologne, who opened doors for me? Did he change or did I change?* Does that even matter?

Still, I hoped, prayed, that when our business started, the business he now insisted on selecting himself without my input, life would get better. It didn't. Ignoring the fact that sharing a business had also been my dream, he continued pushing me away. Like a two-year-old insisting on "doing it himself", the entire subject of "our business" was rife with tension.

The harder I struggled to find a place, a role for myself, in the company Peter purchased, the farther apart we grew. Never letting me forget it was his family who helped put up the money for this venture; Peter rejected all of my "suggestions", my brilliant ideas. We often argued at work. At home, no longer having the subject of my adoption to discuss since my search had come to a dead end, Peter and I had little to talk about. I was realizing this business would not bring us closer together as I'd hoped. Insisting that everything be run his way, not caring about my opinion at all, Peter and I butted heads constantly.

    I still didn't want to give up on my marriage. I didn't want to fail again. What kind of example would that be for Brandon and Katie? I didn't want to teach them that when the going got tough, I quit. I didn't want them to think all marriages went bad. To give up on the hope of marriage in their own futures. But Brandon and Katie had no idea how Peter treated me when they weren't around. How my husband told me to "shut the fuck up" in front of customers. What would they want me to do if they knew the man I chose to be their step-father treated me with contempt? Wouldn't I be setting a worse example staying in a relationship in which I felt degraded?

    I became afraid to open my mouth. If I complained, I was a bitch. If I kept quiet, he knew what I was thinking. Like déjà vu, I heard, "you are...you shouldn't...you never..." No matter what I did or said, I was wrong. Having grown up with an abusive mother, I wanted peace. I knew there was no sense in defending myself. Evenings and weekends I'd spent more and more time hiding in my room, praying my husband would stay away and leave me alone. Complete with TV and food, beverages and bathroom, I was set for days; coming out of hiding only when I was certain Peter was in a good mood. Those times grew few and far between.

    Sometimes, when I got home from work before Peter, I'd sit on my bed, waiting for the garage door to open. I'd hope he'd come upstairs, tap lightly on my door, and apologize. *Joanie, I'm sorry. I didn't mean to take my frustrations out on you. It'll get better. Just wait. You'll see.* That never happened.

    I recalled an important lesson I learned in Al-Anon years ago. I have the right to change my mind. I thought about my situation. If a woman walked into a hospital with bruises all over her body, no one would blame her for seeking help. For finding shelter, protection from her abusive husband. Shouldn't it be the same for a woman who is humiliated every day? For a woman who is put down, told to shut….up in front of others? Who is degraded? Who hides out in her bedroom, struggling to catch her breath, praying her husband will go away? It takes strength to stand up for oneself. It takes courage to leave. To walk away from financial security. To try to make it on my own.

They say "you can only change yourself". Since our previous attempts at marriage counseling did not help, I set out to work on me. Maybe I could fix myself to make my marriage work. Perhaps I might learn a way to express myself so Peter wouldn't feel threatened by my suggestions. Rather than deal with his insecurity, maybe I could learn to rephrase my thoughts so he would no longer take everything I said as a criticism, a personal attack on his intelligence. So he would allow me my opinions without calling me a bitch. I needed to learn how to talk to my husband, present ideas to him in a way that would allow us to work together, with neither of us becoming defensive. I made an appointment with a psychologist who was referred to me by my gynecologist.

There was no time for years of therapy. I needed answers now. I needed to have my problems addressed so I could go back to the office and work with my husband on a day-to-day basis without either of us losing our tempers. I wanted my sessions to get right to the point. I wanted to explain my issues to the doctor and learn how to deal with them. With my notes in hand, I was ready to lie on "the couch" and spill my guts. Channeling Woody Allen's character in *Annie Hall*, I nervously wrenched my sweaty hands clasped tightly in my lap. I took a deep breath, prepared to tell my side of the story.

Yes, this was the moment I'd waited for. I was excited to finally get a chance to talk about me for a change. I'd spent so many years bottling up my thoughts. Never divulging my deep, dark secrets, in fear others would judge me, or worse yet, take his side. I was ready to open up to a stranger about my issues. And if I chose, I could talk about my marriage. The marriage I still hoped to save. There I was, seated upright on the chair next to her desk, instead of lying on "the couch", which, in and of itself, was disappointing. I let the counselor, the expert, begin our conversation. Drumroll please...

"Where are you from?" she asks.

"New Jersey." I answer. I really need to explain to this woman whose face is partially hidden behind a legal pad, that I'm not interested in analysis. I don't have time to go through my whole childhood history. What my parents did and did not do, affecting my self-esteem as an impressionable child, did not matter right now. We can deal with that later. Now, I need to deal with the issues I have today. "Can we talk about the issues I'm facing today? I don't really want to get into my background. I'm having a lot of trouble in my marriage. I need answers."

"New Jersey," she repeats, ignoring what I had just told her. After pausing to take a deep breath, followed by a loud sigh, she adds, "We need to talk about that. People from NJ are..." Did she really say what I thought she said? People from NJ are ...what? Loud? Opinionated? Smart? Attractive? Does she associate everyone in New Jersey with the Mafia? Or with gum-chewing, teased-hair gang members singing and dancing like the Pink Ladies in the musical *Grease*? I don't care about people from NJ. I don't want my issues to be lumped together with every stereotype she's ever heard of people from New Jersey. I'm an individual. I have my own wants and needs. As she lowers her legal pad to her lap, I notice her lips moving but I've tuned her out, not listening to a word she's saying. Maybe she thinks all adoptees are alike. What if I had said I was adopted? Would she assume all my feelings and responses stemmed from my being abandoned by my birth mother? Finally, tuning back in, I hear, "We should set up weekly appointments."

"OK," I respond, agreeing to the same time the following week. I leave her office, angrier, and more confused, than when I arrived. At home, I wait until after six P.M., assuming she'd be gone for the day and won't answer a telephone call. I punch her number into my phone and leave a voicemail canceling my next appointment. That'll teach her.

Not yet ready to throw in the towel on my marriage or our

business, I decided to try to accept Peter the way he is. Controlling. Needing to get his way. Threatened by my asking a question, thinking I'm questioning him. I'd learn to say "yes dear" while doing what I wanted, when I wanted. Hell, I had food on the table. A nice home. I had money. My part-time job allowed me to pay for my children's education. Deciding not to rock the boat should have solved my problems. It didn't. The situation at home got worse.

Taking my new role as a business partner (to him I was a subordinate, but I considered myself a partner) seriously, I felt obligated to "share" my views. And honestly, I would have done everything differently. Some people asked me why I just didn't step away from the business for the sake of the marriage. That was not an option. Having a business was my dream as well. When we were dating we always talked about someday having a business. Losing my marriage meant losing our business. Although I did not want to fail at marriage again, I wanted the business more. It was my career.

As the year progressed, our relationship continued its downward trend. I spent days on end, locked in my room fearing anything and everything I said would be misconstrued. History repeated itself as I sat curled-up, hiding behind my locked bedroom door, listening to Peter's ranting, his raving. His unbridled temper. I'd married a clone of my mother. Again, everything I did was wrong. For my own sanity, I needed to get out. By Thanksgiving, tempers flared and the end of my second marriage was imminent. I had no choice but to end this farce before I lost all my dignity.

Maybe searching for my birth mother was the glue holding my marriage together. When my search had reached a dead end, we found we had little in common. The business that I thought would be ours; never was. Searching my online records while preparing to meet with my attorney, I discovered some of Peter's old emails to his attorneys. In reality, he had begun pushing me out of the business, making it all his, long before any contracts were drawn up. He never had any intention of partnering with me. By the time I put an end to our ten-year farce, the damage was irreparable. There was no turning back, no chance for friendship. I just wanted out.

My second divorce, unlike the quickie dissolution to my first marriage, took years to finalize. During that time I went back to teaching Weight Watchers full time. Barely making enough money to pay the bills, my savings dwindled trying to maintain a mortgage on a house that I couldn't sell until Peter signed the quit claim. As he kept dragging the case through court, his "team" of high priced lawyers insisting he was broke, I maintained my dignity, sitting tall in court, fighting back the tears, trying to emerge with enough money to live on until I could get back on my feet.

Not having to work full-time while married to Peter turned out to be a mixed blessing. It allowed me the freedom, the time, to help my daughter by caring for my granddaughter. However, while other women were working their way up the corporate ladder, I hadn't even reached the first rung. Other than teaching Weight Watchers, I didn't develop any marketable skills. What was I going to do with my life? How would I support myself? Where would I live?

After the divorce was finalized, I was finally able to put the house on the market and plug the enormous drain on my limited finances. For the first time in my life, I found myself looking for a place to live, on my own. Having moved from my parents' house to a dorm, then to an apartment, then a house with my first husband, then living with my children before moving in with my second husband, I'd never lived alone. At a time when I should have been celebrating my freedom, my liberation from emotional tyranny, looking forward to picking out the place I wanted to live, I feared moving backwards.

Without a full-time income, my housing options were severely limited. I dreaded the mere thought of trading in my four-bedroom colonial for a one-bedroom apartment. How could I go back to apartment living after having it all? Why had I refused the diamonds, furs, and expensive cars, rejecting anything ostentatious? I was naïve. I could have sold those baubles and banked the money. Why didn't I use the time I spent cowering in the bathroom, hiding in my bedroom, planning for my future instead of feeling sorry for myself. Why didn't I let Peter pay for the kids' education? He could afford it. Then I could have banked my money and used it to secure myself a better future. Why is my hindsight always so clear when I couldn't see what was happening right in front of my face?

I needed to put the past behind me and move on. After spending a week in bed, I emerged from my self-imposed cocoon a new woman. Determined to learn from my past, I set out to take the necessary steps to get the most from the sale of my house and find a new place to live. Having also had a part-time job selling real estate, I knew all the tricks of the trade. My home would not sit on the market long. I knew how to maximize my return. I got busy. I painted. I repaired. I replaced the ugly carpeting I couldn't stand from the day I moved in. With the house in move-in condition, I got an offer contingent on me moving out it one month. Yes! Again I got busy. I sold everything I didn't need in garage sales. Then I checked out apartments and scoured the real estate listings for small homes and condos, determined to move on with my life.

    No longer walking on eggshells, hiding from an abusive husband, watching my words and keeping my opinions to myself, I set out to find a perfect place to live. Perfect for me.

    I had a feeling this was to be my new home the moment I entered the condo's remodeled kitchen. The glass cabinet doors would showcase my china. The ceramic tile floor would accent my new flea market kitchen table. The white carpeting would highlight my mom's china cabinet and drop leaf table. But the clincher, the point of no return, was when I entered the master bath. Stepping back to admire my new Jacuzzi bathtub, I was ready to sign on the dotted line. I made an offer contingent on getting possession in two weeks.

    Determined to make the condo mine, put my personal stamp on it, I started the painting while the movers were busy schlepping boxes in from the truck. And within two weeks I met the man of my dreams. At least online.

CHAPTER FIFTEEN

I knew the warning signs. What to watch out for. Those red flags that pop up everywhere, the ones I'd ignored in previous relationships, hoping "they'd change" once we were married. Finally realizing it was not my job to fix someone, I resolved to only date men who did not need to be fixed. That meant no alcoholics. No substance abusers. No one who recently lost two hundred pounds. No one who shows frustration when I talk, preferring monologues over dialogues. I would not date someone unemployed, someone who bad-mouths his ex, someone who does not get along with his children, someone who is uneducated, in jail, missing teeth, living with their mother, extremely religious, too old or too young. I became very picky. And I would not date someone who is married. He must be divorced, not merely separated.

That's why his profile never appeared on my jdate.com search that included only single or divorced men. But when Brad's face popped up on my screen, a week after I moved into my new condo, I had to at least talk to him. I was so tired from my move. Painting, arranging furniture, learning my way around my new kitchen, I was done for the day. After relaxing in my Jacuzzi, I tucked myself into my king-sized bed and remained there for what seemed like an eternity, staring at the ceiling. Reading didn't help me fall asleep. Nothing helped. I found the quiet deafening, as I became too aware of the air conditioner kicking on and off and my brand new refrigerator making ice cubes I probably wouldn't even need. I was used to being lulled to sleep by the drone of traffic associated with living on a busy intersection. I tossed, turned, pulled the covers up to my chin, threw them off the bed. I was hot, I was cold. Basically, I was bored, lonely and sleeping was not an option. I got out of bed, shrugged on my robe, powered up my laptop and logged onto my dating site, ready to check out the market. There he was. The man who listed me as a "favorite". I clicked on his profile. He was pretty cute. And educated. And professional. And....separated. Shit. *What the hell*, I thought. *I'm up. What have I got to lose?*

I could tell this "Brad" wasn't a paying member. Was he too cheap to cough up the basic fee or was he unable to commit since he was merely separated, not divorced? If I wanted to learn more about him, I had to take advantage of my full membership and make the first move. I couldn't stand in the way of fate, could I? What are the odds that I'd log on to my computer at the same time he is online, after I'd already gone to sleep? So I instant messaged, "Hi!", and gave him my email address.

I learned quickly this man wasn't interested in chatting online. He didn't want to IM. He didn't want to correspond by email for months until we could figure out if we had some common interests. He wanted to jump into a relationship with two feet. Right into the deep end of the pool. He wanted to call me.

I'm not much of a phone person. After "hello", I often don't know what to say. What if we couldn't think of anything to talk about? I actually accepted a date once with a gentleman just because he couldn't think of anything else to say other than, "Want to go out to dinner Saturday?" I couldn't refuse a phone call. It was set; he would call me the next day after work. I was ready. By ready, I mean I went to the bathroom and had my glass of Diet Coke sitting on my coffee table. Then I waited. At exactly 7:00 the phone rang. "Hello?" I said.

Brad could have been a talk show host. Maybe he watched a lot of Oprah. Or Letterman. I pictured him on the other side of the line, perhaps sitting at his desk, the one in his profile picture, with a cup of coffee in front of him, reading his carefully worded questions off note cards. I imagined him sitting at his computer composing the questions ahead of time. Perhaps he found the questions online in an article titled: *What you need to know about someone before dating.* Since I hadn't prepared any questions of my own, or topics of conversation, I settled in, curled up in the corner of my sofa, and answered with the first thought that popped into my mind.

"Where are you from?" Brad asks.

"New Jersey. But I've been living in the Cleveland area for a long time." *That was too easy*, I thought. *Hit me with a harder question.*

"How many children do you have?"

"Two..." *You should have known that from my profile.* Then he got into politics.

I wondered how I was doing, if he liked my answers. Perhaps I was on my way to winning a new car or a trip to Puerto Vallarta. I realized I needed to turn this query into more of a conversation. So every once in a while I'd ask Brad the same question he asked me. "So, what do you think of..?" Luckily, he agreed with my answers. After long, I realized we were actually hitting it off. I stopped worrying and began to relax.

Even though we hadn't met yet, our phone calls were becoming a nightly event. I don't know if he was concerned because he wasn't divorced yet, or if he'd been married so long he was afraid to get back into the dating pool. That didn't matter. I enjoyed our calls. In fact, Brad and I got along so well on the phone I never wanted to hang up. I looked forward to 7:00 rolling around every day. I was always prepared, having gone to the bathroom and having a beverage at hand, ready to talk for hours.

After a while, I realized that there were other things I

should be doing rather than sitting around talking on the phone all evening. Since I was leading Weight Watchers meetings during the day, I wanted to work on my new house in the evening. I needed to decorate. Therefore, I needed to figure out a way I could talk to Brad and fix up my house at the same time. But I didn't want to miss his calls since they were the highlight of my day.

My solution: multi-tasking. I think I painted the whole living room and dining room holding a paint roller in my right hand and my cordless phone in my left hand, careful not to confuse the two. I ate my meals while talking on the phone, not skipping a beat to clean up my spilled Lean Cuisine lasagna off my white carpeting. The more I talked to Brad, the more I appreciated how in tune we were, often marveling at how we were finishing each other's sentences. Peter hated when I'd, God forbid, interrupt him in mid-sentence, telling me to shut up and let him finish his thought. Yes, I rationalized; it all boils down to perspective. Brad loved how we were in sync. Peter wanted to control the show.

Finally, Brad was ready to meet me. I, however, no longer wanted to meet him. I was afraid. He was too perfect. We got along so well. I didn't want to spoil that. Why couldn't we just continue our phone conversations forever, as if we were having a long distance relationship?

Of course we had to meet at some point. He convinced me it was "like" he had been divorced for a long time, even though the paperwork wasn't complete. I'd heard that before. He told me his ex was seeing someone else. I'd heard that before. He didn't realize that I'd reached the point where I wasn't afraid of him getting a divorce, I was afraid that we got along too well on the phone. What if he didn't like what I looked like in person? What if I didn't like what he looked like in person? What if we met and we had no CHEMISTRY!

We agreed to meet at Panera Bread, for coffee. If we liked each other, we'd get dinner. If we didn't like each other, we might need alcohol. Or just part ways.

The Panera Bread was virtually across the street, a major

street, from my new condo. Brad would be driving. I'd be meeting him at the restaurant. I was walking. I spent all afternoon getting ready, sure that my new date would just throw on a pair of jeans and run out the door. Men. *It's not fair*, I thought, as I pulled out, and rejected every item of clothing in my wardrobe, deciding each and every top made me look fat. The last thing I needed was my date wondering how I could teach Weight Watchers when I was obviously obese. I settled on a black shirt over a black sleeveless turtleneck top. And jeans. Maybe I looked like a black and blue bruise, but I looked thin. Thin enough. After applying an extra two or three coats of mascara and a swipe of long-lasting lipstick, I was ready.

As soon as I finished sprinting across the four-lane street to get to the plaza, I spotted a man, holding a brown-paper-bag covered bottle in each of his hands, exiting what looked like a brand new, state-of-the-art, hybrid car. The car looked cool. And he looked cute. Very much like how I'd pictured him. Above average height, average weight, nicely dressed in dark jeans and black button-down shirt. "Brad?" I asked.

"Joanie?" He replied. "This is for you," he said, handing me one of the bottles.

I smiled, and immediately relaxed. Brad, with the most adorable dimples that I hadn't noticed before, showed up for our date carrying a bottle of wine and a bottle of vodka, for plan "B", in case the date didn't work out and we needed alcohol. Sticking with plan "A", we enjoyed coffee and conversation at Panera and then headed out for dinner at a local Thai restaurant. After a wonderful evening, we headed back to my place where we relaxed, enjoying the bottle of wine, on my sofa. Yes, we had chemistry. And we never stopped talking. To this day, we never stop talking.

When Brad argues, sometimes trying desperately to get his point across, it's not out of insecurity. He doesn't have a deep seated need to have me agree with him. He admires my intelligence and respects my opinions. And sometimes, I win a disagreement. It's his self-assurance that turns me on the most. He admires my brains and a lot more.

I met Brad after I'd basically given up on finding a man I could respect and grow old with. Having just moved into my condo, I was at a point in my life when I was determined to make it on my own. I didn't need anyone to take care of me. I didn't want anyone to take care of me. I had put enough money down on my house that my payments were small, manageable. Even with my part-time job at Weight Watchers, I calculated I could squeak by, perhaps limiting myself to "basic" cable, until I started collecting Social Security. If I got a real job, with benefits, I'd be comfortable. The hard part for me was letting go of my resentment that I no longer had the "career" that I'd always dreamed of. That Peter retained the business we started and I was shoved to the curb. Since I didn't know where to turn for that full time job, I learned to accept reality. I had enough money to live on for years. I shouldn't complain. I needn't worry.

Brad was icing on my cake. Brandon and Katie loved him. Sammi was young enough to accept him. I figured, if I could win over his children, I'd have it made. I think I got off to a good start with Aaron. Amy took longer. That's natural. Why should Brad's daughter accept a woman who, for all intents and purposes, seemed to be trying to replace her mother? But I wasn't. I just wanted us to get along. Live together in peace and harmony like a modern family. OK, I wanted her to love me. I believed that with my love for her father, I would someday win her over.

I knew Brad loved me. However, he seemed reluctant to make another commitment. He was content with our lifestyle. Why shouldn't he be? I was in his house. Very little changed for him. He went to work every day. Same job. Same hours. Same car. Now, with me living in his house, it was almost as if he was back to his old pre-divorce lifestyle. But I wasn't happy. Content. I needed that piece of paper. I needed assurance that he wasn't going to change. That he wasn't going to leave. I know, a marriage license doesn't mean my life would be perfect. It wouldn't guarantee that Brad would love me forever, that he wouldn't turn on me, become a different person that I feared, or dreaded being in the same room with, like my past husbands had.

Although I'd failed in my first two marriages, I wasn't content living on a day-to-day basis, without a commitment, wondering if Brad would leave, or throw me out, the minute I showed my true colors. The minute I lost my temper, as I've been known to do. Who knows? My fears might have all stemmed back to my mother not accepting me for who I was. Only liking me when I smiled, stayed thin. Agreed with her. I wondered if Brad would still love me if I yelled, or put on weight.

By the time Brad finally got around to proposing, after we'd lived together for almost a year, I didn't need another diamond. Married at eighteen, I had a nice little oval diamond engagement ring. Married again at thirty-six I had a pear shaped diamond. I had my mom's engagement ring and I had her diamond necklace. With a collection of jeweled reminders of past failures wedged into coffin-like slots in my velvet-lined jewelry box, the last thing I needed from Brad was for him to prove his love with another diamond. Since I always wanted what my mom had, the perfect marriage to a hardworking, loving man who would give me the world, I chose to embark on my third and final marriage wearing my mother's diamond on my ring finger. Brad agreed, taking me to a local jeweler to have my mother's engagement ring reset.

As they say, we'd been down this road before. Neither of us cared to put on a charade with a formal wedding. We offered to take the kids on a wedding cruise, but not all of them were as thrilled at the idea as Katie was. Therefore, that option was ruled out. We realized this day could be just for us. Why not run away and do it in style?

Now working at a bank, I went to my job that Friday as usual. Only this time Brad drove me, dropping me off, planning to pick me up in the afternoon. My suitcase was carefully stashed in his trunk. I got off work a little early, heading downstairs as soon as Brad called, telling me he was on his way.

We drove directly to the airport, boarded a Southwest plane to Vegas, and settled in, excited about our upcoming whirlwind weekend. When the plane landed, we were surprised to learn we could check-in to our hotel right at the airport. From there we drove directly to the license bureau, giggling like two teenagers, as we waited patiently in line, divorce papers in hand, excited about completing the legal bureaucratic process before embarking on the final step of our journey.

Waking up in our luxury room on the ninth floor of the Paris Las Vegas Hotel and Casino, I was ready to begin my new life. This time I knew I got it right. It was no gamble (pun intended).There would be no arguing on this day. We both agreed the champagne brunch would be a perfect start. Although it was difficult to tear ourselves away from the elegant offerings at the European French village decor all-you-can-eat (of course) buffet, we toasted each other and moved out to the lobby, to wait for our pink Cadillac convertible to pull up in front of the building.

Sweltering in the Vegas heat, we started getting nervous, checking and rechecking our watches, wondering why our ride hadn't yet arrived. Hoping, praying, this wasn't a sign from God. Brad called the chapel. "Where is our ride?" He asked. I was frustrated that I couldn't hear the other side of the conversation. "Uh huh...Uh huh..."

"What?" I asked, getting more anxious. Brad shushed me.

As he hung up the phone, I noticed his lips moving into an upward position. "A limo is on the way."

"Okay, great." I said. "But why the big grin?"

"It's *an air-conditioned limo* since their convertible Caddy is down. In this heat, I'm thrilled."

Fanning myself, I rolled my eyes agreeing, "You bet."

In less than five minutes, a black stretch pulled up in front of the hotel. Not unusual for this neck of the woods. However, instead of a chauffeur getting out to open the door for us, non-other than the King himself, Elvis (an impersonator of course) hopped out and ushered us in to the nice, cool vehicle. I knew this day would turn out perfectly.

As my handsome fiancé and I marched hand-in-hand down the red-carpeted aisle of Las Vegas's Little White Chapel, while our Elvis sang "Love Me Tender", I proudly wore my mom's engagement ring, my daughter's necklace and carried a photo of the woman I considered my birth mother in my purse, all tangible reminders of the strong women in my life.

It wasn't long before I realized my perfect marriage came at a price. When Brad was given the opportunity to advance his career, we both realized that moving from Ohio to Washington, DC, would mean leaving our children behind. Although leaving loved ones was agonizing, the decision to do so was not. We needed his income for our retirement. Since I'd moved for Ryan when he'd lost his jobs, there was no reason why I shouldn't relocate for Brad to help him advance his career. Besides, since I no longer worked at Weight Watchers and I hated my dead-end bank job I had and welcomed any excuse to quit.

Packing wasn't very difficult since it hadn't been that long since I'd moved from my house with Peter, to my condo, then to Brad's house. There were so many boxes I'd never even opened from my last move. Including those pictures. I realized I'd never shown Brad the photos of my dad and Brandon, pointing out how much they looked alike. Brad and I talked about everything. We felt like we knew each so well. He shared the difficulties of his first marriage and I'd gone into painful details about my two misguided marriages. Yet, I'd never really talked about my adoption. I'd never told him what I'd gone through so far to find my birth mother. And I'd never shown my husband the letters my dad sent to my mom during the war. Although I'd saved everything, since I came to a stalemate with Elaine a few years back, all my childhood memories, including hopes of finding my birth mother, were put on the back burner. I couldn't wait for the move so I could unpack my treasure trove and show Brad the project I'd been working on years before we met.

The physical move took a while, but once we'd settled into our new house in Maryland, I set up my dad's kidney-shaped desk in our bedroom, counting on all the letters and photos to still be in the drawers, just where I'd left them. Most were. Some were missing. I tirelessly searched every corner, every drawer, every box and envelop I could find, retracing my years of work, disappointed that I was unable to locate key documents. After a few weeks, gathering together all the papers I could find, I spread them out on my bed, as I'd done so many times in the past and sadly recalled how I'd lost contact with Elaine over the years. She had been so helpful. But we were at an impasse. When Ella's daughter had told her to drop the subject, totally rejecting the idea that I could have been part of Ella's life, or Ella's biological daughter, I let go. I had to move on with my life. I had no choice. Without my original birth certificate, or some other proof that Ella would have been the first name on my adoption papers, had they been completed properly, I gave up my search. That didn't mean that I forgot about Elaine. She had been so nice to me. So helpful. I believed she had helped me find the answers to my questions. We had just reached a point where it was pointless, futile, to continue our what-if's, our maybes.

After having no luck at finding a job in the Washington, DC, area, I finally gave up and began to pursue the career I'd dreamed of since I was a child. I started writing. During our move, I recorded our adventures, documenting the highs, the lows, our triumphs and tribulations, hoping to fictionalize the experiences and turn them into a novel. I loved my new "career". I was a writer, hoping someday to be a "published author". At the moment, that wasn't the important part. What mattered to me was that I desperately needed to accomplish something. Anything. To put a check in my positive column. It wasn't enough to be a cheerleader for Brad's blossoming career. I needed to make my own mark on society.

Given up as an infant, I wanted answers about my birth. I got none. Pursuing leads about my possible birth mother, I reached a dead end. I forfeited my so-called career in my divorce. I had to quit my dead-end job before securing a new, more valuable position. I needed something to call my own.

Writing was it. No one could take that away from me. I was proud as I hammered away at the keyboard, creating a story that was mine. All mine.

Sitting at my laptop, working on editing my first few chapters, I sidetracked, deciding to go back and do a little more research on my adoption. Perhaps there was more available on the Internet now. I checked out Ancestry.com and Googled the New Jersey laws on adoption, hoping they'd changed since I'd last checked. Would I finally be able to obtain my birth certificate without a court order?

I really needed to fill Brad in on my adoption search. Get him up to date. That night, while watching some right-wingers on TV trying, again, to overturn Roe v. Wade, I pressed the mute button.

"It's not fair," I said, taking a deep breath.

"You know they always attack Roe v. Wade in every election. That's what the Republicans do. That's their platform."

"That's not what I'm talking about. You know I believe in Roe v. Wade. If people in one state have the right to have an abortion, it should be the same in each state. Why is our country so divided?"

"OK." Brad wasn't arguing. That's significant.

I grabbed my Diet Snapple and chugged half the bottle. "It's the same with gay marriage laws. If gays can get married in some states, they should be able to get married in every state."

"Yeah, we agree. So what's your point?"

"It's so frustrating. I need to show you something. Hold on." I run upstairs to my office and pull out the summary of the New Jersey adoption laws I just printed. Plopping down on the sofa I start to explain why I feel it's not fair.

"Take a breath," Brad said.

"Listen, I'm really upset about this. I seriously wish we could do something."

"OK, what did you print out?"

"Look at this." I showed him the following printout.

Ohio adoption laws:
Non-identifying information is available to:
- An adoptee who is age 18 or older
- An adoptive parent of a adoptee who is under age 18
- An adoptive family member of a deceased adoptee
- A birth parent of an adoptee who is age 18 or older
- A birth sibling who is age 18 or older
- A birth family member if the birth parent is deceased

Identifying information is accessible to:
- An adoptee who is age 21 or older
- An adoptive parent of an adoptee who is older than age 18 but younger than 21
- The birth parent or adult birth sibling

"You see, if I was born in Ohio, I'd be able to obtain my original birth certificate instead of a bogus one that was written a year after I was born. After my adoption was final. It's not saying Andre and Sylvia Perlmutter are my adoptive parents. It lists them as if they gave birth to me. That's a lie. I just wish I knew the truth. I wish I knew my genetic background. Everyone is dead. Why should they deny me this information?"

"I know you're upset," Brad said, grabbing a diet Snapple for himself. "What does this have to do with Roe v. Wade and gay marriage?"

"That's the point, Brad. I believe that everyone in the country should have the right to a safe abortion, if they choose, and everyone, even gays, should be allowed to marry whomever they wish."

"OK, so what's the problem?"

"For an abortion, if someone in Ohio can't get a legal abortion in their state, they can go to New York. If a gay person wanted to marry, they could go to Massachusetts, where same sex marriages are legal."

"Are you saying the laws should be the same in each state?"

"Definitely! I believe that one state has no right to deny

someone a right that is afforded by another state."

"OK, then what is the issue? I don't know what point you are trying to make." Brad is so smart. Why do I have to spell this out?

"You see, as I said, a gay person could marry in Massachusetts, someone could get an abortion in New York. But I can't change where I was born. If I was born in Ohio, I'd be able to see my original birth certificate. It's not fair. No state should be able to deny me a right afforded by another state, especially if I have no control of the circumstances....you know what I mean, don't you? I don't know how to say it."

"You're saying you're pissed." Is that right?"

"Yes. I'm getting some popcorn. And chocolate. Want some?"

"Do you want to hire an attorney in NJ?" Brad offered.

"I don't think that would help. What, do they want me to prove that I'll die of an unknown disease if I don't know my medical history? Every doctor asks me my medical background. I get sick of telling them I don't have one. I was adopted. I'm sure a medical history is important, but they don't care. The legislators don't care. Governor Christie of New Jersey doesn't care. I read he vetoed the last attempts to pass adoption law regulations."

"Can we watch TV now? I don't think we're going to solve anything tonight," Brad said,

"Sure. I'm pissed."

"I know. Turn up the volume. Please."

"I need to read you my dad's letters from the war. And show you his pictures, and Brandon's pictures. They're cool."

"This weekend. OK?"

"I'd love to show you all my research. I'm not done yet. I'm not giving up."

"I have confidence in you! Can we watch TV now?"

That was nice of Brad to offer to hire a lawyer to take my adoption case to court. It would need to be a class action suit. From what I understand, the courts are not that willing to let out information without a damn good medical reason. The hole in my heart, my lifelong obsession about the circumstances of my birth, my feeling incomplete, most likely wouldn't win over a judge any more than the countless other cases I imagine have gone before the court in the past. If only I was born in Ohio I'd have rights. That's the issue the legislators, the decision makers, don't get. I can't change where I was born.

Working on the novel I'm writing, my mind wanders. I start Googling my birth name, Stamberg, again. It's not insanity; doing the same thing and expecting different results. The Internet changes all the time. Who knows what I could find out? I check out Ancestry.com again. While on the Internet I look to see what Sammi is up to on Facebook. Facebook always suggests people I might know. I'm never interested in any of their suggestions. But I would be interested in people who might be my blood relatives. I enter "Stamberg" into Facebook. Maybe now Iris or Ronnie would be there. It would be nice to know what they look like. I could look like them. I thought I looked like Ella; maybe I look like her children.

I pull out the picture of Ella again. I compare it to the photo of me when I was her age. We look so much alike. I know it.

I go back to my computer and Google Iris. Oh my God. She died. The woman, who might or might not be my half-sister, has died already. I pull up her obituary. She was only in her 60's? Sixty-nine? That must be wrong. She was so young. If this is true, I'd never get a chance to meet her. Anyway, she was the one who was denying my existence. She's not blocking me now.

I go back online, to Facebook, and search Ron, my potential half-brother, and Elaine. Ron is not listed, but I get lucky anyway. A hit! Yes, Elaine is on Facebook! There's even a picture of her, with her husband. Would she remember me? It's been over ten years. I have nothing to lose.

March 3, 2011. It's been many years since you were so helpful trying to help me find my birth family. The only info I had was I was born with the name Stamberg in Northern NJ 1954. There are so many shows on TV helping people find their birth families. I'm afraid there's no hope for me unless I go to court. But probably everyone has passed by now. It's sad. I remember you were so helpful. I hope you and your family are well. My son lives in Tampa. I'm going down to visit him next week. Take care. Thank you again for your help. Joan

Elaine responds immediately!

March 3, 2011. I remember you very well and have saved your letters. I have often thought of contacting you, but hesitated as I didn't know how you would react. You are right, most of the people who know the "true" story have passed on, so you may never know, but one of my Stamberg cousins is convinced that Ella is your mother and Andre is your father. I am happy to hear from you...see that you have remarried...wonder if you are still in Ohio...and wish you well. Happy travels to Tampa. Warmly, Elaine

"I can't believe this." I said to Brad. Remember I told you about that woman who I was writing to about my adoption, about Ella, the cousin. I told you she was the family historian."

"I remember," Brad said. "Is something new?"

"I found her on Facebook. I wrote to her. Elaine not only remembers me, even though it's been over ten years, she's telling me she now thinks that Ella is my mother, and believes my theory that Andre is my father. She not only believes and remembers my story; she is still talking about me."

"You might still learn more."

"I'm not giving up. I'm so excited. I'm going to write back to her again."

March 4, 2011. I would love to keep in touch with you. My email is xxxxxxxx@aol.com. Yes, I remarried and I made a great choice this time! We live in Maryland now, outside of DC. It seems like I have everything in my life except the one thing I need. Closure. I wish I knew the story. I'm thinking of writing a book and making up my own story. Anyway, I thank you so much for your help. I feel you are the lifeline to my past. I still look at that picture you sent me of Ella. I feel I'm looking at myself. I'd love to see more pictures someday. If you want to write to me again that would be great. My husband Brad suggested that we might be able to meet someday, perhaps the next time we cruise out of Fort Lauderdale. Take care, Joan

Our emails continued.

CHAPTER SIXTEEN

After years of corresponding by letter, then by email, Elaine and I had never even spoken to one another, much less met in person. Now living in Florida, she would be visiting her family in Connecticut, and passing through Baltimore. That's less than an hour's drive from my home. Trivial! I offered to meet her for lunch. I can't think of when I'd been more excited and nervous in my life. I entered the date on my iPhone calendar: Lunch with Elaine – August 7, 2011. Note: her cousin Karen would join us.

I admit, I was nervous. It's not every day you get to meet someone you've corresponded with for, how many years? I think it's been about thirteen years, at least. Now that we're living in Maryland and she's visiting relatives in Maryland, how can I not meet her? This woman is possibly the closest person in the world to my birth mother. Perhaps the only person I will ever connect with regarding the circumstance of my existence. I don't know if she has any more information, but I have to give it a try. Now is the time.

    Checking the Urban Spoon app on my iPhone I try to come

up with a restaurant outside Baltimore we might both enjoy. Something perhaps quiet, maybe a diner, or an Italian restaurant. I'd been pretty religious about my vegetarian lifestyle so I scoured the menus trying to find something with food we both would enjoy. I wished she would have let her cousin Karen choose the restaurant. I didn't know the area at all. Brad and I had gone to a Middle Eastern restaurant in the general vicinity one time when we were in the area checking out home theater seating. I emailed that as a suggestion.

That didn't work out. She looked it up and decided it didn't sound great. We went back and forth several times, finally settling on Panera Bread. Her suggestion. She had no idea how perfect that idea was. Why shouldn't the restaurant where I met Brad, whom I'd been conversing with for months before finally getting the courage to meet him, be the same place I meet the woman with whom I'd been corresponding for years? Once again, a coincidence? I don't know. Maybe it was meant to be. Besides, I felt like I was going on a blind date. I was nervous.

This wasn't just any meeting. I didn't think Elaine had a clue how important that one photo she sent me years ago has been in my life. Although she had recently sent me more pictures, it was that one that I'd kept with me all those years. The grainy copy of the woman who could be my birth mother, the one I copied and pasted on the same sheet as a photo of myself at the same age, now worn out, the edges frayed, literally coming apart at the seams. I had the original in my Oreo tin, and a photo uploaded on my iPhone. She was always with me.

There's something about pictures and blind dates. When I met Brad, all he'd seen was my profile picture. It was pretty good. One of my best shots, as a matter of fact. Still, I worried that he wouldn't recognize me. Or worse yet, that he'd be disappointed in how I looked in real life. Accusing me of lying, presenting a photo that doesn't represent the real me.

Again, I was afraid of not matching a picture. But this time, the image was not of myself. It was the one in Elaine's head. The way she always remembered her favorite aunt. I had looked at the image she gave me so often I felt I knew Ella. I was afraid I'd created a distorted reality in my head that no one would concur. I worried that Elaine wouldn't see any resemblance. I feared all of our correspondence over the years had been a waste of both of our time and energy.

All those years of obsessing, staring at the photo, wondering if I looked like Ella, Elaine's favorite aunt. I believed it. Deep in my heart I felt I knew this woman, the woman who stared back at me with my eyes. Yes, I believed we had the same eyes. When I looked at a photo of Iris, her daughter, I saw no resemblance between that woman and her mother. But I definitely thought I resembled Ella. And my father, Andre, of course. In my mind I had Ella's eyes and cheeks. Her smile and her posture. I had my dad's teeth, forehead and his jaw line. Or so I thought. Finally getting to meet Elaine, I start worrying she'll say we were wrong all the time. I don't resemble her Aunt Ella at all. She'll tell me to forget about it. I start to get really depressed, worrying. But that doesn't stop me.

The big day arrives. August 7, 2011. The sky threatens rain. I wouldn't let a little thing like weather slow me down. I'd waited too long for this meeting. According to my GPS, it should take me about forty-five minutes to drive to the Panera Bread near Karen's house. I planned to leave my house around ten-thirty, giving myself plenty of time. Why rush? You never know if there would be an accident. Actually, since I'd been anticipating this meeting for so many years, I'm surprised I didn't get a hotel for the night and camp out. Anyway, I couldn't sleep, waking up around seven in the morning, anxious to get going.

Tiptoeing into the bathroom, I closed the door to my dressing room, hoping not to wake Brad from his sound sleep. Staring into my closet, I agonized over what I should wear. My standard uniform is black. Black top, black hoodie, black sandals, with jeans. Still dressing like a bruise. Elaine told me Ella was a fashion plate. I used to be fashionable. Years ago in high school, I'd worn clothes so fashionably short I frequently got summoned to the principal's office. I guess that was a real long time ago. The most stylish I've been in years involves donning an animal-print scarf. Should I or shouldn't I risk that? No, this is just lunch. I decided to throw caution to the wind and wear a lime green blouse over my black knit top. That's about as colorful and fashionable as I'd go.

I obsessed more about my face. Should I wear my contact lenses? I'd been wearing my glasses more and more lately because my contacts have started bothering me. Without any warning, no matter what the weather or allergy conditions, for some reason, my lenses would fog up, making it difficult to see. But Ella never wore glasses in any of her pictures. Wanting to look more like Ella, I threw caution to the wind and inserted my contact lenses, carrying my glasses tucked away in my purse, for emergency.

I even worried about how I should apply my makeup. Just a little, or go full out with lots of mascara and dark liner. I wanted Elaine to see my eyes. To see if she thought my eyes reminded her of Ella's eyes. I know it's crazy. What the hell, I thought. I applied my makeup as usual. I decided to just go ahead and be me. With contact lenses.

Leaving home by ten-thirty, as I'd planned, I arrived at Panera Bread by eleven-fifteen. That gave me forty-five minutes to kill. I didn't want to go in ahead of time, sit at the table, alone, staring at everyone who walked in the door. Besides, knowing me, if I arrived early, I'd have to go to the bathroom. Sitting by myself, I'd risk losing my table. Or worse yet, Elaine and Karen would walk in when I was in the bathroom and I could miss their entrance completely. Then we'd never find each other.

Recalling I'd passed a Trader Joe's on the way, I backtracked, parked my car, and went shopping. And, of course, I used their bathroom. Shouldn't be a total waste, as my mom would have said. I didn't buy much, not knowing how long the items would stay in the car. In the August heat. I decided to purchase tomatoes.

My sweaty hands were trembling as I pushed the cart up and down each and every aisle, checking out my favorites: my crunchy, salted almond butter, my high fiber muffins. I didn't need to buy them now. I just needed to look busy. Look like I had a purpose to be in the store, not a serial killer planning their next murder. I couldn't believe how nervous I was. I kept thinking about how often I'd looked at the little black and white picture of Ella over the past years. The grainy photo of her looking so elegant as she sat with other family members, people I'd never even glanced at. There was only one woman in that photo I cared about.

After paying for my tomatoes, I returned my cart to the front of the store and got back in my Prius. Then I drove over to my final destination, Panera Bread. I circled the parking lot and positioned the car facing the entrance so I could see everyone that was entering the restaurant, hoping to spot Elaine and Karen walking in. I didn't know what to look for other than two women, alone. No men, no children. It shouldn't be that difficult. Not planning to walk in the restaurant until precisely noon, I still had time

Sitting, hiding, in my car, I watched perhaps dozens and dozens of patrons coming and going. Although I'd seen pictures of Elaine in Facebook, I wasn't sure I could pick her out from the crowd. Still I looked. As it approached noon, I continued glancing at the latest photos of Ella that I'd copied onto my iPhone, knowing this would be the last time I'd wonder if our resemblance was my imagination or if there was a chance I had actually found my birth mother. The woman I'd never meet because she died over twenty years ago. The woman who didn't die during my birth as my mother had told me.

As I waited to enter Panera, my thoughts shifted to my real mom, Sylvia. The woman who raised me. If my theory is true, and Andre, her husband, was my adoptive father and my biological father, that meant my dad cheated on my mother. My dad was having an affair, or a one night stand, with another woman. Was the woman in the picture I've been carrying around for years the face my mom saw each time she looked at me? I started wondering again if my mom knew the story of my birth. Did she ever meet the woman who most likely slept with her husband? Did she see Dad's face when she looked at mine, a constant reminder of his betrayal? Again, I wondered if this was why she always wanted to change me. To make me look like her, not the woman who stole her husband's heart. Is this why she put her foot through the wall when I asked if she knew anything about my birth father? For the first time, I put myself in my mom's place. If this story is true, I finally understand what Mom must have gone through. At that moment, I not only forgave her for everything, I admired her strength for agreeing to raise me.

With ten minutes to go before noon, or high noon as they say in the Westerns, I had a little more time to obsess. First of all, my lenses were already fogging up so I could barely see. Not being prepared with lens cleaner, I popped the right lens out of my eye, spit on it, wiped it with my tissue and popped in back in. That was not the best idea as the lint from the tissue irritated my eye. Next I had to reapply my eye makeup. As long as I was staring at myself in the mirror I pulled out the picture of my would-be birth mother again, and compared my reflection in my rear view mirror to her photo, one last time, before Elaine had the opportunity to confirm or deny a resemblance. Yes, I determined, the turn of my grin was just like hers. As millions have analyzed the Mona Lisa smile, I had stared at Ella's smile so often, wondering if it was my imagination or if we really looked similar. Her hair was thicker than mine, and curly, but deep down, looking at her face, I'd come to feel I was staring at the face of the woman who had given me life.

I regarded my watch and my cellphone. They confirmed what the clock on the dashboard said: it was time to face the truth. There was no putting this off anymore. I needed to get my butt out of the car and get the answers I'd been waiting a lifetime for. I had suggested to Elaine that we meet by the coffee pots since they are always centrally located in Panera Bread stores.

I took a deep breath, grabbed my purse, opened my door, and exited my car, making sure I locked it right away so I wouldn't risk looking foolish returning to the car to check the lock. Next I stood tall and made my way to the front door. I pulled the glass door open and I walked directly up to the coffee bar, scanning the room to see if I could spot Elaine either entering or sitting at a table.

Not two seconds passed before a short, blonde woman raced up to me, her welcoming arms outstretched, ready for a hug. "Joan?" I nodded, tears filling my eyes at once.

"Oh my God," Elaine said. "I would have recognized you anywhere. You look just like Ella." We hugged. I cried.

She couldn't possibly know how that one sentence validated my entire life. In one solitary instant I was completely absolved of "killing" my mother in childbirth. I now know for certain I was not the product of rape. And yes, I do look like the woman whose picture I'd been carrying around for years as if it were my lifeline, my connection to humanity. My reason to go on. Permission for me to be a part of the human race. I felt I now have a history. I became whole. This was only the beginning. I needed to learn more.

Following Elaine to our booth, I wiped more tears from my eyes before she introduced me to her cousin Karen. I wondered why I had even bothered with makeup at all as the three of us sat in silence for a few moments, the two women staring at me in awe. I clasped my tissues, not ready to speak. Finally, Elaine and Karen nodded at each other, then at me, confirming that I indeed resembled Elaine's Aunt Ella.

Before we began our conversation, I noticed Karen was dressed in all black. I wished I'd stuck with my favorite color instead of choosing green. Although Elaine looked lovely in her green and blue outfit, I was out of my element. Why did I think I should try to be someone I'm not? The glasses, the contact lenses, my clothes. How could I judge and try to emulate someone's entire life and personality based on a few pictures I carry around with me?

While I had spent much time thinking about if Ella could have been my birthmother, so had Elaine. I had to remember, all these years I was basically accusing her favorite aunt of infidelity. Now, I was expecting her to confirm our suspicions.

Across the booth from me, both women, sitting side by side, were staring at my face. I felt uncomfortable and excited being the object of such scrutiny. I'm always self-conscious about my wrinkles, the hairs that I might have missed plucking, my frown lines. Suddenly, Elaine starting pointing at me. With her index finger, she was actually pointing at my face. I guess this instance would be the exception to the "pointing is rude" rule. Then I realized she wasn't pointing at me. She was "pointing out". Pointing out similarities between Ella and me.

With her finger remaining in position right in front of my face, Elaine started pointing at my mouth. Or was it below my mouth? Oh no, she's looking at those lines. Those horrible lines that, years ago, started out as smile lines, have turned into deep folds that people refer to as marionette lines. I hate them. Why is she staring at my absolute worst feature? I'd been desperately trying all the creams and gels on the market to firm up this area but have been unsuccessful. I've already asked for a referral for a dermatologist to get Rejuvaderm or Restylane to fill in the creases. I'm embarrassed that someone, a stranger, is scrutinizing my face.

"My Aunt Ella had the same lines on her face."

At once, this feature I was so ashamed of, my imperfection, became my badge of honor. This isn't a flaw. This is my inherited feature. I inherited this "feature" from my birth mother. My beautiful birth mother. Again, how my life would have been different if my "characteristics" were considered unique, or beautiful, rather than flaws needing correction. Why couldn't my mother tell me my nose was perfect as it was rather than saying I shouldn't wear my hair parted in the middle because it made my nose look bigger?

I couldn't eat one bite of the Caesar salad I chose from the menu behind the counter. Listening to Elaine sated me as if it was my first real meal after years of starving. Better than any frozen yogurt or chocolate cake I'd ever savored.

Taking a moment to get to know one another before diving deep into our respective theories of my birth, Elaine shared with me how she too was nervous getting ready to meet me.

How she obsessed about what to wear and how they arrived at the restaurant very early as well. We were very much alike. I felt like I'd always known this woman. And as a matter of fact, I had known her for quite a while. Just not in person. This meeting was worth the wait.

Time seemed to stand still as Elaine revealed more information than I expected. Ella's daughter, Iris, who was sixteen at the time of my birth, who I thought had denied that her mother was pregnant, never actually denied my possible existence. In fact, she had actually told Elaine to "tear up my letters and never mention this again".

I also learned about another cousin of Elaine's. This one recalls visiting her Aunt Ella during the summer I was born. And she remembers the year because it was the year she was a freshman in college. More proof. She commented that Ella, who was a thin woman, a woman who enjoyed dressing up, a fashionable woman, was wearing muumuus that summer. On top of that, Ella's husband, a gambler, was out of town all summer. Unable to cover his gambling debts, he was hiding from "The Mob".

"Ella's husband was involved with the mob?" I repeated, making sure I understood what she was telling me.

"Yes. He was a gambler. And a ladies' man. Because he owed a lot of money that he could not pay back, we now know he was definitely out of town during the summer you were born. He never would have known if Ella was pregnant."

"Wow." I'm trying to take this all in without making any judgments. Here was a woman, taking care of two children, a teenager and a young boy, and she is coping on her own with her husband away. Running from the mob. She was probably afraid for his life. Hell, she was probably afraid for her own life and her children's safety. I've watched enough *Sopranos* episodes and gangster movies to know these people didn't fool around. And in those days, there were no disposable cell phones that he could have used to tell his family he was all right. Or text messages to keep in touch. For all Ella knew, her husband could have been dead. Who knows how long he was gone? Or if he was ever coming back. She had to go on with life. She had to live.

"And there's more." Elaine added. "Ella lived on Lyons Ave."

"My father worked on Lyons Ave. I knew she lived in Irvington, but I didn't know she actually lived on Lyons Avenue."

"She lived in an apartment above a store."

"Wow. My dad's store was 751 Lyons Ave. They must have known each other. He had a small grocery store. The only grocery store in town, other than a supermarket that was much farther away."

"She lived at 714 Lyons Ave."

"Oh my God." I punched the Google Maps app on my iPhone and typed in both addresses. "Ella lived less than 500 feet away from my dad's store! That's not that much more than the length of a football field." I put down my phone. I looked up at Elaine and Karen. "And my dad offered free delivery. I have no doubt at all she shopped at my dad's store." At this point I'm trembling again. If I had any uncertainty at all before, it was gone. What do they say on TV? Means, motive and opportunity? She was so close to his store, of course she shopped there. Probably every week. Then, when her husband was away, she was most likely lonely. She was a beautiful woman. My dad was a handsome man. Her name happened to be the same as my dad's mother's name. There are too many coincidences for this theory not to be true. My mind was racing. I had to slow down, take a deep breath, a sip of my Diet Coke, calm myself, so I could hear what else Elaine was telling me. I'd already pushed away my salad.

"I have some more information," Elaine said. "The family had a shoe store in Bloomfield."

"I remember, as little girl, Mom taking me to Bloomfield to shop for my shoes. I never understood why we went so far from home, for shoes." I started thinking about how I was jealous of all the other girls who got to wear sneakers when I had to wear dressy Mary Janes and saddle shoes. "I'm just overwhelmed. I can't believe this. I mean I do believe this."

"I have no doubt you are Ella's daughter," Elaine said as the three of us pull out more tissues to wipe our eyes. Anyone would have assumed we'd just left the theater after seeing a tear jerker like *Steel Magnolias*. I was both happy to feel I finally knew the truth and sad that I will never get to meet this woman. And, I'll probably never know the true story. Were my dad and Ella in love? Did my mom know? Did they ever talk about divorce? Was it a one night stand? So many questions. So few answers.

With the preliminaries out of the way, the question: *Am I Ella's child*, answered to our satisfaction, we relaxed a little and started picking at our salads. "How was your parent's marriage?" Elaine asks me. "Did they love each other?" That question took me by surprise. Before this meeting, my answer definitely would have been "yes". Now, I have no idea. I hesitated a moment, thinking about what I should say.

"That's a tough question to answer. I always thought they had the perfect marriage. Now, I'm not so sure." I start thinking back to my parent's relationship. I always thought they had the perfect marriage. It was the marriage I wanted. They were always throwing parties. We had fabulous holidays. Dad went to shul; Mom stayed home and cooked the meal. That was good, wasn't it? Wasn't that how other families lived? The dad went out, the mom stayed home and cooked. Just like *Father Knows Best*. Real life.

Now I'm recalling how Dad always complained that "everyone else's wife was at shul but not my honey child." I knew that upset him. Dad and I would always walk to services together. Sometimes Mom would join us later. She drove. He didn't like that. Were they happy? I don't really know. I don't recall actual affection. I don't remember seeing them hug or kiss. Or even hold hands. I just figured they didn't do that in front of me. I can't remember seeing them exchange gifts. But I know Dad bought Mom jewelry. Charms for her gold bracelet. And she had a diamond necklace that she liked. She wore it all the time. While I'm pushing my salad around on my plate I keep analyzing my parent's relationship. I don't even remember them sitting together watching TV. I just thought that was because she wasn't interested in baseball. Mom listened to the radio while Dad slept in front of the TV. I assumed that's what married couples did when they'd been together a long time. They did watch Johnny Carson together.

"I wonder if Mom knew about the 'other woman'," I said.

"She might have."

I wanted to know everything about Ella. I wanted to know what she did with her time. Did she work? Did she play cards with the girls? Did she smoke? Was she funny? Did she have a sense of humor? Was she caring? Loving? I'll never be able to see her mannerisms, hear her voice. I'd hoped I'd get some stories. I asked Elaine the questions I had jotted down on a note card.

"She baked banana bread," Elaine told me. "Do you bake banana bread?"

"Yes! I have baked a few banana breads in my life!" Banana bread! Proof we are the same blood! We have something in common. Or not.

My drive home seemed to take longer than my drive to the restaurant. I was frustrated by the traffic. The weather threatened rain. My GPS was acting up, recalculating several times for no apparent reason. I couldn't wait to talk to Brad. To tell him what happened. He wasn't with me in the beginning of my adoption journey, but he was my cheerleader through the homestretch. When I called to tell my husband I was on my way home, I wanted to let him know about what I believed was the most important lunch/meeting of my life. I wanted him to know that, although I feel I got the proof I wanted, I still craved more. Although I knew Elaine couldn't give it to me, I still wanted a story. At best, I'd hoped for a love story. What I got was a preponderance of evidence. With all the facts I'd learned, I was confident I had enough information, details, that would have been sufficient to make a case in a court of law. For a jury to vote in my favor in a civil trial. However, this was not a court of law. And I was not a defendant, or accuser. As Elaine told me during our early correspondence, she and her sisters were romantics. She wanted to learn the story. So did I. Since I still hadn't learned how my dad and Ella grew close, the minute I pulled into my garage, while still in the car, I typed, as a note on my iPhone, my version of how Ella and Andre met. Then I emailed it to Elaine.

There was no doubt she was beautiful. He was not sure if he was drawn to her rich brown eyes or the way her lip curled slightly as she spoke to him. He couldn't take his eyes off that face as she placed her grocery order. An order for her family. Her children. She's married. She made that clear. In that moment of time it didn't matter. He was glued to her every word. "I'll need your name and address. I'll personally deliver this to your house right after work," he said with all the charm of Fred Astaire asking Ginger Rogers for her hand at the ball.

"Oh, I live just a few doors down."

"And your name is?" he added with a wink, the blue dominating his hazel eyes.

"Ella. Call me Ella."

Andre's heart skipped a beat as if he hadn't heard correctly. It hadn't been that long since his mother, Ella, was sent to Auschwitz. He stopped for a moment, unable to write.

Ella, noticing the tear in his eye reached for his hand. "What is it?" she asked.

Andre couldn't answer. Ella waited, her hand grasping his tighter. Their eyes met.

"My mother. I tried to save her. I didn't reach her in time."

CHAPTER SEVENTEEN

Brad and I were planning a cruise in December, choosing to sail out of Ft. Lauderdale, Florida, so we could visit Elaine at her home in Boca Raton, after we returned to port. During this visit we looked forward to meeting Elaine's husband, Don, and the woman, the famous cousin "Lois" I learned had visited Ella during the summer of 1954. The summer when this hip, vibrant, attractive, dare I say sexy woman, was wearing muumuus. Although her aunt being pregnant didn't occur to her at the time, looking back now, she insists this must be the case. According to Elaine, Lois had been home from college. Since she was a freshman at the time, she remembers the year, and confirmed that Ella didn't look her usual slim self. She could very well have been with child. Although I was already convinced I'd found the answer to my lifelong question, convinced I knew who my birth mother was, I hoped for more confirmation. Lois was the one other person who could validate what Elaine and I believed to be true.

After years of research, years of letters back and forth with Elaine, years of obsessing about my birth, in my mind everything was riding on this one meeting with Lois. During most of our ten day cruise my mind was preoccupied. Would she concur? Would she agree with Elaine and me that Ella was my birth mother? Would she think I resembled Ella? I was so nervous. Almost as nervous as I had been meeting Elaine.

December 8, 2011

As expected, after travelling from port to port throughout the Caribbean, the cruise line threw us off the ship at the crack of dawn. We had made reservations at a local hotel with a confirmation that our room would be ready for an early arrival time. We would be tired after the long voyage. Although Elaine offered to pick us up from the cruise port, Brad and I planned to take a taxi to the hotel, hoping to be able to freshen up before visiting. Besides, we didn't want to put her out any more than necessary. She'd been so helpful already.

When we learned that the taxi ride to the hotel would set us back around $100 for a one-half-hour trip, we took Elaine up on her generous offer. "I'll be there in a half an hour. Look for the 'Giants' license plate," she told me when I called.

"OK. Can't wait! Thank you so much." To help spot us in the crowd I added, "I'm wearing an orange hoodie."

How could I have known that all the port workers would be dressed in orange? After several more phone calls, and a lot of waiving, we spotted the correct license plate and prepared to start the next leg of our journey.

Elaine was her bubbly self. She was so excited to see me again, and thrilled to meet Brad for the first time. By now, she was referring to me as her cousin, or cuz for short. She dropped us off at the Hampton to freshen up and arranged to pick us up in an hour. That was perfect. Although exhausted from the trip, we were high on adrenaline. I could tell Brad was as excited as I was.

The three of us went directly to "the club" (the restaurant at the condo's golf course) for lunch, where we met up with Elaine's husband Don. After a quick bite and a chance to get to know each other a bit, we all drove back to Elaine's condo, which was exactly how I pictured it would be. Just like the set of *The Golden Girls*, it had a bright, airy, and cheery feeling. Neither Brad nor I had ever felt so welcomed in our lives. Basking in the glow of the Florida sun, and being with the woman who has devoted a good deal of her thoughts to my inner well-being, was beyond description. I was standing in the home of the woman who personified the very definition of *mensch*: a person of integrity and honor. Elaine truly cared about me. Not because she had to. Because she wanted to. She is a great person. She is my new family. Yes, my cuz.

Again, as I had been nervous meeting Elaine for the first time, I worried about meeting Lois that evening. I didn't have a clue what she would remember. We didn't have a history of letters going back and forth as I had with Elaine. I didn't know what Elaine had told her other than Ella most likely gave birth and put the child up for adoption. *And guess what, we are having dinner with that child tonight.* This could be a new spin on *Guess Who's Coming to Dinner*.

Lois and her husband Louis arrived at six, just as planned. We all stood in the foyer, greeting each other with pleasantries. Saying our, "Hellos". They asked us "How was your trip?" "Fine," we answered. Then Elaine and Don played host and hostess, taking drink orders and carting plates of hors d'oeuvres to the coffee table. After Elaine refused my offer to help, Brad and I retreated to the living room where we huddled close together on Elaine's pristine white sofa, a piece of furniture that would have been chock full of food stains had it been in my house. I was careful not to spill anything.

Lois and Louis were charming. Socializing, with drinks in hand and tempting treats at arm's length, Brad and I enjoyed the schmoozing, feeling like we'd just gone back in time. With a Jewish/Italian *Mad Men* vibe, since they were drinking Scotch and Manhattans, I felt like I was with family. Being nervous, I stuck with my Diet Coke. I really needed to keep my wits about me.

First came the small talk. The weather. More questions about our cruise. I was surprised no one was saying/asking anything about me. I thought I was the guest of honor. The subject of the evening. The one in the spotlight. I expected an interrogation. "So what makes you think...?" "How dare you...?" No one even mentioned Ella. They just acted as if I belonged. As if I was a long lost relative, maybe one who had moved to California. Who had been away for years. We talked as if we were all just catching up. I didn't detect any awkwardness on their part, as if we were meeting for the first time. Other than my inner butterflies, which would be unusual if I didn't feel that way, the situation felt great, natural, and strange all at once.

After a while, I'd heard enough talk of sports. I didn't care about the scores of games. Or politics. We could talk about all that later. Although I was becoming frustrated, I kept it to myself. I kept smiling. However, I was dying to know what Lois thought. When she looked at me, did she think I resembled Ella? Did she believe the story that Elaine and I had been working on for years. *Enough of the cheese, the crackers, the chocolate. What do you think, Lois?*

"Lois," Elaine said, finally. "What do you think of Joan? Do you think she is Ella's daughter?" Now, all eyes were on me. I held my breath, waiting for the official verdict.

Lois merely shrugged the question off matter-of-factly as if she was saying the sun will come up tomorrow. "Of course she is." Immediately the conversation reverted right back to the weather, the news, politics, now the Republicans... Obviously, in Lois' mind, there was no question. I was Ella's child.

As the conversation got back to Ella and my story again, Lois would refer to Ella as "your mom". I was taken aback. *No*, I wanted to say. *Sylvia was my "mom," Ella was my birth mother. Don't they know that?* Soon, it was no longer about me at all. It became Ella's story. This was the part I wanted to hear. The part I'd waited years to hear.

According to Lois, Ella was not happy with her husband, her marriage. He was a gambler, a drinker. The mob was after him. Ella donned a brave face and stayed married. When her husband left town, the family helped her out financially. I guess that's what they did in those days. This was the whole story. All

Lois knew for sure. The rest was up for speculation.

Everyone decided then and there that Ella had fallen in love with my dad. That "Ella and Andre" was a love story. I was a love child. Again, my eyes welled as Elaine and Lois summed up my life. I grabbed a tissue from my pocket and dabbed away the tears as I listened to these two women agreeing, "She could have gotten an abortion," Lois said. They nodded to each other.

"We knew others in our family who got abortions." Elaine added. "We believe she knew Andre had been trying to have a child. We believe she kept the pregnancy so he could have a child." Wow! I like that. I was a gift.

All my life, over fifty years of thinking I'd killed my birthmother. Thinking I was the product of rape. The secret that my mother couldn't bear to share was that my father was in love with another woman. That's the secret she carried to her grave. I understand now. I forgive her. Now I can let go. Almost. We all went out to dinner at a local Italian restaurant chain. After Lois and Louis went home, Elaine confided in me that Lois said, "Ella would have been proud."

Deep breath. I was losing it again.

Now that we were as certain as we could be that I am Ella's daughter, I told Elaine I wanted to meet my brother. I knew Ella's daughter Iris, who had passed away, never wanted to acknowledge me. But what about that little boy? The one who would have been a seven-year-old at the time of my birth? If Ella is my birth mother, this man would be my brother. *I have a brother!!* I didn't know if he would even believe that I was his sister. If he would want to meet me. But I had to try. I had to find out. I asked Elaine if she would contact him for me. Find out if he has any interest in meeting his sister. Elaine said she would talk it over with her husband and son to see if they thought that would be a good idea.

Brad and I had already returned home. Tired from our recent adventures, we just hung out in front of the TV. Chilling. Brad had the whole weekend to relax before he had to return to work on Monday.

The following day I received an email from Elaine saying

she and Don, as well as their son, agreed that contacting Ronnie would be the right thing to do. I hoped Ronnie would feel the same way. It's funny. Although he is actually seven years older than me, I still picture him as a little seven-year-old child. Who knows? He could totally reject me. Dismiss even the possibility of having another sister. Especially since the sister he'd grown up with had recently died. Maybe he didn't want a replacement sister showing up out of nowhere. I had to try. I'd wanted a brother my entire life. I just got one. The plan was for Elaine to contact her cousin first. By email. Then by phone. And if he agreed to speak to me, she would let me know. Elaine copied me on her email.

On December 14, 2011, Elaine sent an email to Ronnie:

> Email to Ronnie:
> Subject: Hello
>
> Hi Ronnie, It's Laney. How are you? It has been a long time. I would prefer writing to you by "snail mail", but I wasn't sure of your address. I hope this finds you well. The family is shrinking, and it really is sad that we lost my dad, the last of the "original Stambergs". Meanwhile, I have a VERY SENSITIVE subject to discuss with you. I don't know if you even want to discuss this. I had (sort of) mentioned it to Iris some time before she passed away, and she told me to forget about it and never bring it up again!! I can't, however, continue to "harbor" a secret that you may not be aware of. I hope you are sitting down. Here goes: Ron, I believe I have met your half-sister! I have been in touch with a lovely young woman who believes that Aunt Ella was her birth mother and that she was adopted at birth. This woman has done a lot of research and the "clues" she has unearthed are too many to be coincidences. I met her last week, and both Don and I saw your mother in her face!! If you want to pursue this, I would be more than happy to

share more details and put you in touch with her. If you want nothing to do with this, so be it. I will tell you that she is really nice, is after nothing but closure, and is aware of you (the Internet) and would love to meet you. I will be awaiting your response. Meanwhile, I want you to know that I think of you often. I sincerely hope that you are well and still can burp those vowels. Love you, little cousin. Love, Laney

Response from Ronnie:

Hi cuz, wow how are you?? How is Don and your kids?? Well I have so much to tell you.

Ronnie filled Laney in on what's been going on in his life. He'd been having medical issues and does not have access to a computer right now. He's borrowing a friend's computer to answer this email.

Yes I would love to meet my half-sister. Wow Wow Wow. My cell no is 614 xxx-xxxx. Call me anytime and we can talk and I can explain all about me to you. Stay well and take care. Hope to hear back from you very soon. Love you very much. Always, Ronnie. Thank you again for the email. Call me.

Since we are now officially cousins, I asked Elaine if I could call her Laney and told her to call me Joanie. After she got Ronnie's email, she forwarded it to me adding:

Joanie - OMG - What do you think? Love, Laney
PS If you want to continue this, don't you think I should call him first???? What should we do????
I replied:

Yes, definitely, call.

Saturday morning, I sat glued to my cell phone. I kept it

next to me, plugged in, charging, so I wouldn't risk running down my battery while waiting for Laney's call to tell me how her conversation went with Ronnie. The phone finally rang.

Although anxious to jump in with questions, I remained silent, listening with awe as Laney replayed her amazing conversation with my half-brother. According to her, this man had no doubt she was telling the truth. He believed her story without question. Although he has few memories before the age of twelve, she told me, he said he does remember going to André's Meat Market. A lot. She said she gave him my email address.

Maybe that's why Mom was always mean to me, having Dad spank me when he got home from work. She was punishing him and me for my origins. I thought it was normal for a mother to say "your daughter". Maybe she meant it literally. Maybe she knew. She must have known.

I expected to get an email from Ronnie right away. If he was anything like me, he'd be anxious to learn more. I kept checking my messages, disappointed to find nothing. After I hadn't heard from Ronnie in a few days, I couldn't wait any longer. I emailed him.

December 29, 2011

>Dear Ronnie. This is Joanie. Elaine, Laney, told me that she told you about me. She said that you were very accepting of my existence and the probability that we are related.
>
>A little background: I've been curious about my birth all my life, as most adoptees are. My mother had always told me my birth mother died in childbirth and she didn't have any info about her. After my mother died in 1988 I found my adoption papers with the name Stamberg and learned my birthmother didn't die in childbirth. I was told she handed me to my father, which sounded strange to me. Years later I

found a picture of my father as a teen and he looked identical to my son as a teen. I started wondering if my adoptive father, Andre Perlmutter, might have been my birth father.

Years later I found Elaine through a letter writing campaign and I found the name Ella Stamberg online. Ella, who had already passed away, had my birth name and my same middle name. In addition she lived on the same street as my father's store. There were so many coincidences. The biggest coincidence was how much I looked like Ella. Not exactly, but in the pictures I have there is a very strong resemblance. NJ doesn't allow adoptees to obtain their original birth certificates but after 13 years of research Elaine, Don and Lois agree that I must be Ella's daughter. I told Laney that I'd really like to meet you if you were interested. I was thrilled when you seemed to welcome the idea. I understand you are moving soon. My children live in Ohio. I'd be happy to drive to Columbus sometime during one of my visits to the Akron area.

I'd love to hear from you. I never wanted to intrude but I'd be thrilled to learn more about you and about Ella. I'm so excited. I look forward to hearing from you soon.
Joanie

There was still no answer. The New Year came and went. No word from my brother. On January 11, I sent him another email, referring him to my last email. He responded immediately.

Hi sister. How are you? I have no computer since I moved. Soon I hope. Feel free to call me... Want to meet you. Was never told about you. OMG. Want to see you in person. Cannot wait. Love you. Always,
Ronnie.

Unbelievable. He gave me his phone number. He seems to accept that I'm his sister. No questions asked. How about that for unconditional love!

I tapped the underlined number the minute I got his email on my iPhone and the phone started ringing. He picked up almost immediately. Speaking to my brother (*my brother!!!*) was the most natural thing in the world. I felt like I'd always known this man. We connected in a way that is rare for me.

First we touched on the basics. That I tried to contact the family many years ago. Ronnie said he bets Iris knew their mother was pregnant since she was a teen at the time. He said he went to Andre's Meat Market all the time. He gave me the names of some of Ella's friends. He was in the Air Force. He's in a lot of pain. He assured me that I didn't need to worry about inheriting Ella's heart problems. They were the result of a childhood illness. I shouldn't worry about the diabetes either. That's from the Stamberg side. We talked and talked. Nothing earth shattering, merely bantering back and forth as if this wasn't strange at all. As if this was our regular weekly call, just two siblings catching up on what we did over the holidays. Only we weren't catching up on the holidays. We were trying to make some sense of our lives. That's a big difference. But it didn't feel that way. It felt strangely normal. I couldn't wait to meet him. We'd plan a trip to Columbus after there was no more chance of snow.

April 13, 2012 – Friday. I hardly slept at all last night, finally drifting off around five in the morning. I was nervous. I couldn't stop wondering what my brother would be like. Would we have anything in common? Maybe share the same nose. The same hairline. Even the same, or similar voice. I can't tell from the old pictures I have of him.

I've also been wondering if I blew my one opportunity for a grand entrance. I could have called a local news station. I could have publicized my story. Where was Oprah when I needed her? But I'm shy. Maybe my brother is shy as well. This is best done in private. I don't know. I don't know anything more than we share the DNA of one woman.

Lying in bed, I reminded myself this is not a segment of a TV show. This is real life. I'm not looking for ratings, for advertisers, for sponsors. I just want to meet the man who I still picture as that boy of seven, the age he was when I was born. The age he was when his sister, at sixteen years old, most likely knew her mother was pregnant. I can't worry about that. With a long day ahead of us, I was glad I had Brad with me for support.

Brad and I got up early for our drive to Columbus. I usually let him use the bathroom first, but I was anxious, jumping out of bed a minute before the alarm went off. I looked out the window and checked the weather app on my iPhone. Slightly overcast. A perfect day for a drive.

It felt strange preparing my car for this trip. We've gone to Ohio so many times since moving to Maryland. Visiting the kids. Brad's mom and sister. We always pack some snacks and beverages, planning to stop at the service plazas on the interstate for lunch. Even though we were going to Ohio, Columbus seemed like an entirely different destination than the Cleveland area. We didn't know where we would be stopping for lunch, or my important bathroom breaks. Normally these changes would have been exciting. Part of the adventure. But this time was different. I just wanted to get the drive over with. This one time, it wasn't the journey. It was definitely the destination. I was anxious to meet my brother, at last.

The drive turned out to be long and uneventful, stopping only for a quick sandwich at a Subway and an extra bathroom break. Brad and I kept glancing at the GPS as it counted down the miles, indicating we were nearing our destination. It also helped break up the monotony of staring at the long, winding highway. Rather than our usual banter, discussing politics or my reading funny jokes from my iPhone apps, we remained quiet. There was nothing left to say. Having already discussed all of our what-if's, we were at the goal line. I was about to get closure on the question I'd been asking my entire life. "Who am I?" Cliché? Yes. Still, this was important to me.

Brad and I planned to check into our hotel and freshen-up in our room before meeting Ronnie in the hotel lobby. We would then go over to the Bonefish Grill, down the street, for dinner.

Even though he wouldn't admit it, I sensed Brad was as anxious as I was as we walked hand-in-hand down the hotel stairs, ready to make our grand entrance, as if we were the guests of honor at a party at The Ritz, not a neighborhood Hampton with comfortable beds and a free breakfast buffet.

We hadn't realized we'd be entering the lobby from the rear. Ronnie, at least I assumed it was he, was standing with his back towards us, looking up at the flat screen TV hanging from the wall. In a loud whisper, I called out his name. As if I was watching a dramatic scene from a Lifetime Original Movie, this man seemed to turn toward me in slow motion. Tears welled in my eyes as the room faded away and I ran to hug my brother. MY BROTHER!

Like so many reunions I'd seen on TV, mine was as unbelievable. Only without the camera crew. It was better that way. We both felt a sense of urgency, a physical need, to catch up on a lifetime of wasted years. Years in which neither of us knew the other existed.

We found a little table by a window and the three of us prepared to settle in. Brad, not quite ready to relax, got up to fetch a few cups of coffee from the bottomless pot in the lobby. I waited for my husband to return before I started to speak. As he handed me my beverage, I was glad to have something warm to hold on to. To help calm me down. My hands trembled and I'm sure my voice was shaky as I looked into my brother's eyes and started my first in-person conversation with a sibling. "My mom lied, telling me my birthmother died in childbirth."

"It was a lie of omission for me," my brother added. "I'm sure my sister knew. She had to." We learned a lot about each other over the course of the evening. We'd both gone from marriage to marriage, perhaps searching for something that wasn't there.

My brother, *my brother*, had been a world-ranked bowler.

One of the best in the country! I wanted to see his pro shop. I wanted to feel his pride.

The following day brought another joyous occasion. As my brother held my hand, measuring me for a bowling ball, I finally felt complete. Whole.

Many years ago I had attended a local blood drive and registered as an organ donor. As the years passed, I'd often fantasized about getting a call, learning that I was a perfect match for someone who desperately needed an organ. Perhaps a kidney, or partial liver. Like in the movies, or afternoon soap operas, I imagined I'd discover we were siblings. Or even twins, separated at birth. Now I didn't have to wait, wonder if there was someone out there who shared my blood. I asked my brother his blood type. "A+."

"Same as mine!" I knew we'd be a match!!

I couldn't wait to fill Laney in on our meeting.

Hi Laney,

I wish you could have been with us when we met since you made it all happen. Ronnie said he spoke with you. I don't know if he called you or if you called him. He is so happy to have a sister! It's unbelievable.

He texts me constantly. The only question he seemed to have was why did we wait so long to tell him. I told him Iris told you to drop the subject. Then we lost touch for years. I told him it was not until after we got back in touch years later that we started putting more pieces of the puzzle together. And that's when we realized his dad was away. And the information from Lois. I told him that we wanted to let him know as soon as we were sure.

It's interesting. He says his dad was away from home for over a year. That even makes the story more plausible. It's very understandable that a woman, whose husband is gone, not knowing when or if he's coming back, or if he's dead or alive, would find comfort in the arms of another man. Everything fits together. It all makes sense.

The three of us went out to dinner. The following day we went to his pro shop. He's so proud of his bowling record, and he should be. Few people have a natural talent like that.

He's so happy and I'm so happy that we put the pieces together.

That would be so great if he could come visit here when you, I hope, stop by, or stay here, on your way to Connecticut.

Everything is so great! I'm thrilled. But the fact that my brother is so thrilled makes everything we've gone through worthwhile!!!
Can't wait to see you! Love to Don!
    Love Joanie

Now, for the icing on the cake: I get one of many texts from my brother:

Hi sis. Forgot to tell u. We met on Friday the 13th. Mom was born on Friday the 13th.

That is so cool! I always notice dates. I'm really into numbers like that.

I text back:

There's more: we met on the 13th. Her birthday was on the 13th day in 1913!!! Thirteen is now my lucky number!!

EPILOGUE

In reality, I was born on a Monday. Dad was probably at work. Born in Newark, New Jersey, the Beth Israel Hospital was right down the street from Dad's butcher shop. If I was born during the day, Dad might have gotten the call at work, flipped the "open" sign to "closed" and went directly to the hospital, arriving in time for my birth. Maybe he was with Ella, holding her hand during her labor. Maybe my mom didn't want to come to the hospital at all, arriving later, at her leisure, to help carry me in the car. I'll never know what really happened that day. *She handed you to your father,* started all of this. I still have unanswered questions. Does it really matter at this point? Everyone who would know the answers are gone. Even the sister that denied my existence has passed away. Did she ever tell her husband? Did Ella's husband know? Secrets. They can kill. Even though I'd love to see my original birth certificate, I need to let go now.

    I now know my roots. I have closure. That will have to be enough. Yet, there is still an emptiness I can't explain. Along with my understanding of why my mom couldn't tell me the truth, and why my dad never said a word, I have a profound sadness for everyone involved. Mom didn't show her love for me until after my dad passed away. She held in so much anger when in fact, she was a hero for raising me. How many women would do that? I feel sad for my dad not being able to tell me the truth. I'm sure he wanted to. I wonder what would have happened if Mom had passed away first. I'll never know. I need to put this to rest. I need to move on. So many secrets. Very sad.

ACKNOWLEDGEMENTS

I want to thank all the people who stood by me while I was searching and encouraged me to keep going. To never give up. My husband. My children, step children and granddaughter. I want to thank my mother, the woman who raised me. I want to thank the woman who gave me life. I can't give enough thanks to Elaine, the "romantic" who helped me piece together the puzzle of my existence, and to my brother, Ronnie, who accepted me into his life with no questions asked. And I want to give a special thank you to my creative step-daughter Amy Kaufman for designing the cover of this book.

ABOUT THE AUTHOR

Joan E. Kaufman is an author, adoptee and healthy-living proponent. Ms. Kaufman currently lives in Maryland and is also the author of *Who Moved My Cookies?,* available on Kindle, Nook and iBooks.

For more information please visit:
www.joanekaufman.com

Made in the USA
Columbia, SC
20 January 2025